COUNSELING FOR DIVERSITY

A Guide for School Counselors
and Related Professionals

Courtland C. Lee
Editor
University of Virginia

Allyn and Bacon

Boston • London • Toronto • Sydney • Tokyo • Singapore

Library of Congress Cataloging-in-Publication Data

Counseling for diversity: a guide for school counselors and related professionals /
Courtland C. Lee, editor.
   p.   cm.
   Includes bibliographical references and index.
   ISBN 0-205-15321-6
   1. Educational counseling--United States   2. Minority students-
-Counseling of --United States.   3. Multiculturalism--United States.
I. Lee, Courtland C.
LB1027.5.C65   1994
371.4'0973--dc20

94-2860
CIP

Printed in the United States of America

10 9 8 7 6 5 4 3   98 97 96 95

To my grandmother, Elizabeth M. Wheeler,
for her nearly a century of
insight and wisdom about people

CONTENTS

0394893

PART II   *Culturally Responsive Counseling K–12   19*

PREFACE

American society has been transformed over the past four decades. The 1954 *Brown* v. *The Board of Education* Supreme Court decision and the social turmoil of the civil rights movement in the 1960s helped to foster a new awareness that the United States is a culturally diverse society. The concept of cultural diversity has received its impetus not only from the *Brown* decision and the major economic, legislative, and social gains made during the civil rights struggles of the 1960s but, more recently, from changing population demographics. Significantly, projections of the U.S. population into the twenty-first century indicate that people of color will experience a substantial rate of growth while the white population will decline significantly. In addition, over the next 20 years this country's population will be increased with large numbers of immigrants from nonwestern parts of the world. This immigration phenomenon will bring significant numbers of people with new world views into the United States.

Cultural diversity has become reflected in the American educational system. Data suggest that schools are currently populated with students from increasingly diverse cultural backgrounds. This diversity presents educators with unique challenges. This is particularly true for school counselors and related professionals who must promote academic, career, and personal-social development within the context of diverse cultural realities.

Counseling for Diversity: A Guide for School Counselors and Related Professionals is an attempt to meet the challenges associated with school counseling and related student development practice in a culturally diverse society. The authors who have contributed to it have done extensive consulting with school systems throughout the country on issues associated with multicultural counseling. It is evident to us that there is a pressing need among professionals at the elementary, middle, and secondary school levels for practical ideas on how to manage a multicultural counseling program.

This book provides practicing school counselors and their colleagues in related professions with direction for developing, implementing, and evaluating important components of counseling programs for culturally diverse student groups. It is also designed to be a useful methods textbook in school counseling, school psychology, and school social work training programs.

FOCUS OF THE BOOK

The focus of *Counseling for Diversity* is on developmental counseling in culturally pluralistic school settings. Intervention strategies and techniques for counseling, consultation, classroom guidance, and coordination for promoting the development of racially/ethnically diverse student groups are offered. In addition, the book provides direction for evaluating the effectiveness of culturally responsive developmental counseling programs.

OVERVIEW OF CONTENTS

In Chapter 1, "School Counseling and Cultural Diversity: A Framework for Effective Practice," Courtland C. Lee explores school counseling from a developmental perspective with a focus on how cultural dynamics are important considerations for promoting educational and social success. He also lays a foundation for planning, implementing, and evaluating culturally responsive school counseling services.

Part II of the book consists of five chapters on individual and group counseling methodologies for promoting the academic, career, or personal-social development of specific racial/ethnic student groups. The interventions presented in these chapters are derived from both the professional and personal experiences of the chapter authors, who are either members of the specific group examined or have an intimate working knowledge of a particular group.

In Chapter 2, "Counseling Interventions with African American Youth," Don C. Locke examines elements of African and African American cultures and how they affect the education of African American youth. He offers specific guidelines for counseling with this student group and also describes two secondary school projects designed to enhance the education of African American students.

Morris L. Jackson provides several case studies that offer direction for counseling intervention with Arab American children and adolescents in Chapter 3, "Counseling Youth of Arab Ancestry." In addition, he discusses important aspects of Arab and Arab American family life, religion, values, and their relationship to the psychosocial development of young people.

In Chapter 4, "Counseling Asian American Students," Darryl Takizo Yagi and Maria Y. Oh present an awareness-, knowledge-, and skill-based approach to counseling students from this cultural background. A special focus on counseling Korean American students is offered, as well as direction for working with young people who are recent immigrants from Southeast Asia.

Jesse T. Zapata offers comprehensive techniques for working with Hispanic students in Chapter 5, "Counseling Hispanic Children and Youth." He discusses the diversity found within this cultural group and the variables that promote the development of Hispanic young people.

Part II of the book concludes with Chapter 6, "Counseling Native American Students." In this chapter, Timothy C. Thomason discusses some important dynamics to consider when working with young people from this cultural group and provides direction for implementing a school counseling program for Native American students. He also provides direction for both individual and group counseling with Native American youth.

Part III provides direction for culturally responsive consultation, classroom guidance, coordination of counseling services, and counselor accountability in the school setting. In Chapter 7, "Cross-Cultural School Consultation," Carol F. Duncan provides a definition for consultation and a framework for considering this process in a cross-cultural school context.

Michael M. Omizo and Michael J. D'Andrea, in Chapter 8, "Multicultural Classroom Guidance," offer direction for conducting classroom guidance activities that promote concepts of cultural pluralism and an appreciation of diversity among children.

In Chapter 9, "Coordination of Counseling Services in a Culturally Pluralistic School Environment," Johnnie H. Miles provides background information and strategies that focus on the coordination role of school counselors in a pluralistic educational environment. She presents an explanation of the dimensions of coordination, which is the newest of the school counselor roles. In addition, she offers case scenarios to introduce the practical contributions that coordination can make to counseling programs in culturally pluralistic school settings.

Arleen C. Lewis and Susanna Hayes, in Chapter 10, "Accountability in a Culturally Pluralistic School Setting," focus on the basic elements of accountability and how to conduct needs assessments, program development, and evaluation in culturally pluralistic school settings.

In the concluding chapter, "Multicultural Literacy: Imperatives for Culturally Responsive School Counseling," Courtland C. Lee examines aspects of professionalism that are essential for the development of culturally responsive school counselors. He offers suggestions on how school counseling professionals can engage in an ongoing professional and personal development process to gain new awareness, knowledge, and skills related to issues of cultural pluralism.

ACKNOWLEDGMENTS

I would like to thank a number of people whose efforts have made this book a reality. My sincere appreciation to the authors who contributed the chapters. I am grateful to them for their hard work in putting their creative ideas and practical experiences down on paper. Thank you for taking the time to share your knowledge about and commitment to cultural diversity.

I am grateful to Mylan Jaixen, executive editor at Allyn and Bacon, for believing in this project and giving me encouragement to undertake it. Likewise, I appreciate all the help provided by Sue Hutchinson, editorial assistant at Allyn and Bacon, on the technical aspects associated with the production of the book.

A special note of thanks must go to the reviewer who critiqued the first draft of the manuscript, Mary Bradford Ivey, Amherst (Massachusetts) Schools. I greatly appreciate your constructive feedback on the manuscript; it has made this book much stronger.

My heartfelt thanks to Michelle "Missy" Sirch, my graduate editorial assistant on this project. Without her able assistance in keeping the files, maintaining the flow of correspondence, and keeping a watchful eye on the day-to-day details, the book would not have been completed.

A special note of gratitude must go to Theresa Michie, Robyn Nelson Jackson, Andolyn Saunders, and Edith Simms, who assisted in the typing, proofreading, and final preparation of the manuscript. I am most appreciative of all your efforts. Thank you for pitching in.

Finally, a special word of thanks to my wife, Antoinette, whose love, support, and understanding were a constant source of inspiration throughout the development of the book.

Courtland C. Lee

ABOUT THE EDITOR

Courtland C. Lee received his Ph.D. in counseling from Michigan State University. He is a professor and director of the Counselor Education Program at the University of Virginia. His areas of research specialization include multicultural counseling and adolescent development. He has published numerous articles and book chapters on adolescent development and counseling across cultures. He is also the author of a book on counseling African American males. Dr. Lee is editor of the *Journal of African American Male Studies*, former editor of the *Journal of Multicultural Counseling and Development*, and serves on the advisory board of the *International Journal for the Advancement of Counselling*. A former school teacher and school counselor, he has served as a psychoeducational consultant to educational institutions and has conducted professional development workshops on multicultural issues both in the United States and abroad.

ABOUT THE CONTRIBUTORS

Michael J. D'Andrea received his Ed.D. from George Peabody College for Teachers at Vanderbilt University. He is an assistant professor with the Department of Counselor Education at the University of Hawaii, Manoa. Currently, he is involved in a number of projects in the Hawaii public schools, running counseling programs designed to promote students' moral and social development.

Carol F. Duncan received her Ph.D. in school psychology from the University of North Carolina at Chapel Hill. She is a licensed practicing psychologist and the clinical coordinator for Children and Youth Services at the Orange-Person-Chatham Mental Health Center in Chapel Hill, North Carolina. She is an adjunct professor within the School of Education at the University of North Carolina at Chapel Hill. She also works as a private practitioner. She has interests in cross-cultural consultation, training, and service delivery.

Susanna Hayes received her Ph.D. from the University of Michigan. She has worked as a school counselor and teacher in Michigan and Washington. She is currently an associate professor in the counselor training program at Western Washington University and is an associate of the Center for Cross-Cultural Research.

Morris L. Jackson received his B.S. and M.Ed. from the University of Hartford and his Ed.D. from George Washington University. He has also studied the Arabic language and culture at the King Saud University of Riyadh, Saudi Arabia. He is educational director of the Office of Continuing Studies at the American University in Washington, D.C. He is also an adjunct professor of Counseling at the Bowie State University and Virginia Polytechnic Institute and State University. Having traveled throughout Europe, Northern Africa, the Middle East, and the Carribbean, he has interests in cross-cultural counseling and training and has provided consultations to both the private and public sector.

Arleen C. Lewis received her Ph.D. from the University of Nebraska at Lincoln in clinical psychology. She is an associate professor and director of the M.Ed. program in school counseling at Western Washington University. She is a licensed psychologist and an associate of the Center for Cross Cultural Research at Western Washington University.

Don C. Locke received his B.S. and M.Ed. from Tennessee State University and his Ed.D. from Ball State University. He is professor and former head of the department of counselor education at North Carolina State University at Raleigh. He is a registered counselor and a licensed psychologist and has provided consultation on multicultural issues in Germany, Holland, and throughout the United States. His current research interests are in the areas of cognitive development and African American development.

Johnnie H. Miles is an associate professor of counselor education at Virginia Tech, Falls Church, Virginia. She received the Doctorate of Education from Auburn University and has been employed as a professional counselor. Her primary interests are career development and cross-cultural communication and counseling. These themes have been central to her work in teaching, research, and consulting.

Maria Y. Oh received her B.A. from Indiana University and her M.Ed. from the University of Virginia. As the counseling unit manager at the Korean Youth and Community Center, Inc., in Los Angeles, California, she is responsible for the development and coordination of child abuse and juvenile delinquency prevention and intervention projects for Korean American youth and families.

Michael M. Omizo received his Ph.D. from the University of Southern California. He is a professor at the University of Hawaii, Manoa, in the department of counselor education. He is currently doing research on homeless children, wellness promotion for elementary school children, and counseling terminally ill children.

Timothy C. Thomason received his M.A., Ed.S., and Ed.D. degrees from George Peabody College. He is a licensed psychologist and associate professor of educational psychology at Northern Arizona University. He is director of training at the American Indian Rehabilitation Research and Training Center and director of adult programs at the Institute for Human Development in Flagstaff, Arizona.

Darryl Takizo Yagi received his B.A. from the University of California, Berkeley, and his M.A. in counseling psychology and M.A. in Special Education from the California State Universities, Chico and Sonoma, respectively. He has been an elementary and junior high school counselor, and is currently a high school counselor as well as a licensed marriage, family, and child counselor in private practice. He has provided counseling and consultation on cross-cultural issues in Japan and throughout the United States.

Jesse T. Zapata received his B.A. from the University of Texas at Austin, his M.A. from Texas Tech University, and his Ph.D. from Arizona State University. He is an associate professor in counseling and guidance in the division of education and director of the Hispanic Research Center at the University of Texas at San Antonio. He is a licensed psychologist and has research interests in counseling issues regarding Hispanics.

P A R T I

INTRODUCTION

1

SCHOOL COUNSELING AND CULTURAL DIVERSITY: A FRAMEWORK FOR EFFECTIVE PRACTICE

COURTLAND C. LEE

"What is multicultural counseling? How is it different from any other form of counseling?"

"Do I really need to view minority students as being different from white students? Shouldn't race or color be unimportant in working with children?"

"Can a counselor from one race *really* counsel a student who is from another race?"

Questions such as these are often asked in workshops on multicultural counseling conducted with counseling professionals in school systems throughout the United States. They illustrate the frustration these individuals often experience as they attempt to address the academic, career, and personal/social concerns of increasingly diverse student populations.

Among the contemporary issues facing school counselors and related helping professionals, addressing the developmental needs of the growing number of students from culturally diverse backgrounds is, perhaps, the most challenging. Estimates are that by the year 2020, the majority of school-age children in the United States will be from racial/ethnic minority groups (Hodgkinson, 1985). A review of public elementary and secondary school enrollment trends by race/ethnicity for the period 1985 to 1995 by the Western Institute Commission for Higher Education and the College Board (1988) indicates that during this period, white students, while still a majority, will be a smaller proportion of the overall elementary and secondary school population. White enrollments are expected to decrease from 71 to 66 percent.

Conversely, Asian/Pacific Islander enrollments in the nation's schools are increasing more rapidly than any other group—more than 70 percent between 1985 and 1995. Latino/Hispanic enrollments are also increasing rapidly (more than 54 percent), from 3.3 million to 5.1 million during this period. African Americans are still expected to be the second largest racial/ethnic group among enrolled students. Finally, Native Americans, although the smallest racial/ethnic group, will still experience a 29 percent increase in enrollment.

In concrete people terms, data such as these mean that, as never before, U.S. schools have become a social arena where children who represent truly diverse behavioral styles, attitudinal orientations, and value systems have been brought together with one goal—to maximize their potential as human beings (Lee, 1989). Cultural pluralism, therefore, has become widely recognized as a major factor deserving increased understanding on the part of educators. In the midst of such sweeping demographic changes, school counselors must provide comprehensive services that promote student development. Significantly, the American School Counselor Association has established a position statement on cross/multicultural counseling that calls for the facilitation of student development through an understanding of and appreciation for cultural diversity. This statement encourages school counselors to take action to ensure that students from culturally diverse backgrounds receive services that foster their development. It outlines a series of strategies for developing the awareness, knowledge, and skills necessary for promoting cultural diversity within the school environment and beyond (American School Counselor Association, 1988).

However, there is a growing realization that current services often do not have broad applicability across the range of cultural backgrounds represented by students. School counselors are becoming increasingly aware that their practices are rooted firmly in the values of European, European-American middle-class culture, whereas the cultural values of a significant portion of their student clientele represent world views whose origins are African, Asian, Mexican, Central American, Caribbean, or Middle Eastern. With this awareness brings a frustration that in attempting to promote student development, the values inherent in counseling and those of culturally diverse students often come into conflict in the helping process (Lee, 1989).

This frustration is compounded by the fact that many school counseling professionals have received little or no systematic training in multicultural counseling (Carey, Reinat, & Fontes, 1990). This is because such training is still a relatively new curriculum dimension in most counselor education and related training programs (Ibrahim & Thompson, 1982; Ponterotto & Casas, 1987).

In order to resolve this conflict and the frustration that often accompanies it, cultural differences must be effectively addressed in the provision of school counseling services. It is evident that counseling professionals need a framework from which to operate if they are going to ensure that students from culturally diverse backgrounds have access to services that promote optimal development.

This chapter provides such a framework. It explores school counseling from a developmental perspective with a focus on how cultural dynamics are important considerations for promoting educational and social success. The chapter also lays the foundation for planning, implementing, and evaluating culturally responsive school counseling services.

DEVELOPMENTAL SCHOOL COUNSELING: A MULTICULTURAL PERSPECTIVE

Developmental Counseling Defined

In order to build a comprehensive school counseling program that meets the needs of a culturally diverse student body, it is important to develop a conceptual base for such a service. According to Myrick (1987), both *guidance* and *counseling* are terms used in the school setting to delineate services offered to students that focus on academic, career, and personal/social development. For Myrick, the major organizing principle for such services is *promoting human development*. Specifically, developmental counseling focuses on life stages, characterized by student abilities, interests, and needs, as well as helping students learn life management skills (Myrick, 1989). Developmental counseling programs focus on student competencies and outcomes. The principle of developmental guidance has been advocated as a major thrust in organizing school counseling programs for several decades (Dagley, 1987; Dinkmeyer, 1966; Mathewson, 1949; Muro & Dinkmeyer, 1977; Muro & Miller, 1983; Wrenn, 1962). Significantly, incorporating developmental concepts into the school counseling role has been repeatedly supported by the American School Counselor Association (1978, 1979, 1981, 1985). In essence, this association has stated that developmental counseling is for all students and its purpose is to facilitate optimal personal development.

An important role for a school counseling professional is to facilitate student movement toward developmental goals. Axelson (1985) has succinctly defined developmental activity desired in counseling experiences:

1. *To help the person evolve the possibilities in his or her personality;*
2. *To help the person draw from his or her natural resources and strengths;*
3. *To help make something available or usable that the person needs;*
4. *To help the person move from a present position or situation to one providing more opportunity for effective use by the person;*
5. *To help something unfold gradually for the person;*
6. *To help the person grow and differentiate along lines natural to what the person is or wants to be;*
7. *To help the person acquire something that the person needs or wants;*
8. *To help the person expand by a process of growth. (p. 11)*

It seems apparent that an understanding of the dynamics of human development is crucial to helping young people achieve academically, make career choices, and attain intra- and interpersonal adequacy. If, as has been stated, developmental counseling is for all students, then, given demographic realities, the process of human psychosocial development must be considered within the context of cultural diversity as it relates to the dynamics of race/ethnicity. Specifically, culture needs to be understood in terms of the developmental dynamics of those young people from racial/ethnic groups who trace their cultural origins to places outside of a Western European, European-American conceptual framework.

Psychosocial Development and Cultural Diversity

Theorists and researchers have suggested that major aspects of human psychosocial development unfold in a series of life stages and are influenced by both heredity and environment (Erikson, 1950; Havighurst, 1972; Kohlberg, 1966; Piaget, 1970). As individuals progress through the life stages, they must master a series of developmental tasks. Mastery of tasks at one stage of life influences success with those in succeeding stages. This success contributes to the formation of all aspects of human thinking, feeling, and behaving.

In a developmental framework, school counseling professionals are confronted with the challenge of helping young people master the tasks of childhood and adolescence. Understanding the developmental dynamics of these two life stages is basic to effective school counseling.

Childhood can be characterized as the stage that forms the foundation for human development across the life span. The early part of this period is characterized by mastering fundamental skills such as walking and talking. Developing skills in reading, writing, and calculating mark the latter part of the period. Childhood is when human beings, through family interaction, develop a sense of trust and autonomy. In addition, through mastery of basic skills, children develop a sense of initiative and industry. Childhood is also when individuals learn social skills that involve relating emotionally to the family, adults, and peers. Acquisition of such skills is an aspect of developing attitudes toward social groups and institutions (Daehler & Bukatko, 1985; Kessen, 1965; Miller, 1983; Piaget, 1987).

Adolescence, the next life stage, marks the developmental transition between childhood and adulthood. This period is characterized by significant physical and psychological changes. It marks a sudden increase in body size and strength, as well as a change in many physiological functions, including reproductive capacities. It also marks major personality changes designed to attain self-identity and meaningful independence (Elkind, 1984; Erikson, 1965; Offer, Ostrov, & Howard, 1981; Rice, 1990).

Although there seem to be universal aspects to the phenomenon, social and behavioral scientists have indicated that the process of psychosocial development may need to be revised when considered across cultures (Mead, 1928; Munroe & Munroe, 1975; Powell, Yamamoto, Romero, & Morales, 1983). It has been suggested that this process is subject to considerable racial/ethnic variation in its behavioral manifestations, its symbolic meaning, and its societal responses (Phinney & Rotheram, 1987). Children and adolescents must master psychosocial developmental tasks through their socialization within a cultural context. This refers to social environments, such as family and community, and their patterns of interpersonal relationships that impact affect, behavior, and cognition (Koss-Chioino & Vargas, 1992). Through family and community interaction, the beliefs, values, social forms, and material traits that comprise cultural realities are passed from older generations to younger ones.

Racial/ethnic variation in the cultural context of families and communities can be observed along various dimensions, some of which will now be discussed.

Notions of Kinship
There appear to be important cultural differences in the emphasis placed on bonds of interpersonal affiliation established within family/community kinship networks. In some cultural traditions, a major emphasis is placed on the nuclear family and individual autonomy; whereas in others, great importance is placed on extended family kinship networks and interdependence among individuals. This individualistic versus communalistic distinction in kinship social organization can affect the development of perceptions and attitudes regarding relationships with individuals, social groups, and institutions among young people.

Roles and Status
Cultural differences exist with respect to roles and status within families and communities. Central to this are prescribed notions or traditions concerning individual responsibilities and obligations that are based on age- and/or gender-defined roles and status. Children and adolescents are socialized into roles and assigned status within a family/community hierarchy based on such notions.

Sex-Role Socialization

There are cultural differences concerning perceptions of the role of males and females. Differential gender perceptions can influence the expectations considered normal for psychosocial development. Such expectations may account for fundamental differences in personality development for boys and girls in the traditions of many cultures.

Language

Acquisition and use of language is an important aspect of socialization for young people. Mastery of language often fosters success in future developmental tasks. Children are socialized into a language tradition at an early age. There are, however, significant cultural differences in language traditions, as well as the value placed on specific language use. Personality development in childhood and adolescence can be significantly impacted by distinctions in language traditions. This is particularly evident when there is a conflict of cultural perceptions regarding differences in language traditions and value.

Religion/Spirituality

Religion and spiritual influences are universally important in shaping the formation of behavior and values in young people. However, there are significant cultural differences in the extent to which such influences may impact childhood and adolescent psychosocial development. The distinctions between religious and secular life vary across cultural groups. The degree of such distinctions among families and communities can significantly affect aspects of personality development.

Ethnic Identity

Dynamics such as those just given, when considered in total, contribute greatly to the development of an ethnic identity among young people. Ethnic identity is the primary principle for understanding psychosocial development in a cultural context. According to Phinney and Rotheram (1987), "ethnic identity refers to one's sense of belonging to an ethnic group and the part of one's thinking, perceptions, feelings, and behavior that is due to ethnic group membership" (p. 13). It can be considered as the inner vision that one develops of oneself as an *African* American, *Arab* American, *Korean* American,

Mexican American, *Native* American, or *Italian* American. Ethnic identity greatly influences psychosocial development, particularly in a culturally pluralistic country such as the United States. The manner in which young people come to view themselves in relation to members of their own cultural group and members of other cultural groups can significantly shape aspects of personality (Phinney & Rotheram, 1987).

Ethnic identity development has spawned significant scholarly interest in the field of multicultural counseling. Experts have conceptualized and investigated the process by which ethnic minority individuals develop an ethnic identity (Atkinson, Morten, & Sue, 1989; Carter & Helms, 1987; Parham & Helms, 1981; Phinney & Rotheram, 1987). Within the body of knowledge on ethnic minority identity development can be found ideas that suggest there is significant intergroup variability with respect to individuals' sense of belonging to an ethnic group and the part of people's personality that is directly attributable to ethnic group membership. This knowledge base focuses on the concept of ethnic minority identity formation and the possibility that people of color go through a series of stages in their efforts to establish stable personalities within U.S. society (Atkinson, Morten, & Sue, 1989).

Perhaps the most famous approach to understanding ethnic identity development was conceptualized by Atkinson, Morten, and Sue (1989). They suggest that identity development for racial/ethnic minority group members progresses through a series of stages that reflect a person's view of self, others in the same minority group, others of another minority group, and those in the majority group. Atkinson, Morten, and Sue have applied this notion to produce a model of minority identity development. The stages of minority ethnic identity in the model include:

Stage One: Conformity   A minority group member thinks, feels, and acts in ways that are suggestive of a preference for the macroculture value system. An individual at this stage has a negative view of his or her own culture and often rejects his or her ethnic heritage.

Stage Two: Dissonance   A minority group member experiences events that create dissonance in the primacy of his or her macroculture world view. An individual also begins to question the nature of the rejection of his or her culture of origin.

Stage Three: Resistance and Immersion   A minority group member acts, feels, and thinks in ways that reflect unequivocal acceptance of one's own culture and a complete rejection of the macroculture.

Stage Four: Introspection Stage   A minority group member begins to reflect on and become concerned about the nature of the unequivocal acceptance of one's own culture and the rejection of the macroculture.

Stage Five: Integrative Awareness   A minority group member acts, feels, and thinks in ways that reflect selective appreciation across cultural groups. At this stage, an individual accepts his or her ethnic heritage and develops a selective acceptance of the macroculture.

Environmental Factors

The complexity of the cultural context in U.S. society is often further compounded by several important social environmental factors. As Koss-Chioino and Vargas (1992) have suggested, these factors are often interrelated and must be considered major variables in psychosocial development in a culturally pluralistic society. These social environmental factors include:

1. *Racism*   As a social environmental phenomenon, racism can adversely impact psychosocial development. Racism is a pattern of discrimination and prejudice between one group who is idealized and favored and another group who is devalued and exploited solely on the basis of race in a common relationship (Pinderhughes, 1973). The extent of the impact differs, however, in significant ways, depending on the particular racial/ethnic group young people belong to and whether that group is in the majority or minority. For both ethnic minority and majority youth, the effects of racism may severely undermine the cultural dynamics associated with ethnic identity development.

2. *Economic Disadvantage*   Poverty affects racial/ethnic groups disproportionately. For many groups of people, poor housing, inadequate schooling, and low-quality health care impact negatively on most aspects of family and community life. The forces of economic disadvantage can converge to impact negatively on the psychosocial development of children and adolescents. Economic disadvantage can negate the cultural context and impede the emergence of a climate that is conducive to the successful mastery of developmental tasks.

3. *Acculturation*   Acculturation, within the context of American society, refers to the degree to which an individual identifies with the attitudes, behaviors, and values of the predominant macroculture (Lee, 1991). These attitudes, behaviors, and values reflect the cultural traditions of middle-class Americans of European origin. The acculturation process differs in significant ways, again depending on the particular racial/ethnic group young people belong to, and whether that group has majority or minority status in society. Acculturation may present a major developmental challenge to young people from an ethnic minority group. Social and economic success are often predicated on an individual being able to adopt the lifestyle of the macroculture. Young people from ethnic minority backgrounds must master the task of balancing an ethnic identity with one that will ensure success in the macroculture. In many instances, young people can find themselves caught between two cultures.

Although this list of dimensions associated with the cultural context and key social environmental factors is by no means exhaustive, an examination of pluralism in the United States would indicate that these are some of the salient influences on psychosocial development. They can significantly impact on the mastery of key developmental tasks throughout childhood and adolescence. If school counseling professionals are to meet the academic, career, and social needs of young people from increasing diverse backgrounds, then such dimensions and factors must be understood and considered in the helping process.

School counselors and related helping professionals who work with students from diverse cultural backgrounds must facilitate the developmental process within a myriad of cultural contexts. Developmental school counseling must, therefore, be predicated on an understanding of cultural dynamics and their crucial impact on psychosocial development.

DEVELOPMENTAL SCHOOL COUNSELING AND DIVERSITY: THE CHALLENGE

School counseling that is predicated on an appreciation of cultural diversity and that prepares young people for meaningful lives in a pluralistic society can provide a direct service not only to students but to educational professionals and communities as well. Such a service must include the primary roles of the contemporary school counselor, variously established as *counseling, consultation,* and *coordination* (American School Counselor Association, 1990; Myrick, 1987). Additionally, this service must be held accountable for its objectives, procedures, and outcomes. The major focus of these activities should be to facilitate self-understanding, interpersonal relationships, and problem-solving/decision-making skills related to the educational, personal/social, and career development of students from culturally diverse backgrounds. Adopting such roles in a multicultural context requires concerted effort and careful planning. The challenge lies in defining roles that will comprise culturally responsive school counseling services.

Counseling

Counseling involves interactions between counselor and students where they work together on issues or concerns. Through individual and group counseling, as well as large-group guidance interventions, culturally responsive counselors should be able to help students from a variety of racial/ethnic backgrounds develop healthy self-concepts and learn to respect cultural diversity, while setting educational, career, and personal/social goals.

Consultation

In addition to direct intervention with students, culturally responsive counselors should be able to consult with fellow educators and parents to develop a supportive network for all students. Working with other educational professionals, counselors should promote awareness of and appreciation for cultural diversity as a way to enhance the learning process. Likewise, counselors should help bridge potential gaps between parents and the school by examining ways to incorporate the inherent cultural strengths of families and communities into the educational process.

Coordination

Comprehensive school counseling should also involve managing a variety of indirect services that benefit students and serving as a liaison between school and community agencies. Culturally responsive counselors should, therefore, have a working knowledge of the resources and agencies available in diverse communities that can be enlisted to meet the specific needs of young people.

Accountability

School counselors should engage in evaluation procedures to assess the effectiveness of their program planning and implementation. These procedures should include gathering data from students, school personnel, and parents about the stated goals and objectives of the program and whether these are culturally responsive. The analysis of such data should serve as the basis for making culturally appropriate changes in counseling services.

The remainder of this book is devoted to ideas for addressing the challenges associated with developing, implementing, and evaluating comprehensive multicultural school counseling programs. School counseling professionals, in their various roles, should work cooperatively with individuals and organizations to promote the overall development of young people from diverse cultural backgrounds.

CONCLUSION

Although there may be questions raised and frustration expressed by school counselors attempting to address the educational, career, and personal/social concerns of students from diverse cultural backgrounds, the major demographic changes impacting the nation's schools present these professionals with a great opportunity. Perhaps as never before, school counselors and their colleagues in related professions have the opportunity to carefully redefine and articulate their roles and functions. This redefinition and articulation, however, must be based on a commitment to help all students master the important developmental tasks of childhood and adolescence. It must also advance efforts to organize programs and provide interventions that focus on needs and issues related to diverse cultural realities.

REFERENCES

American School Counselor Association Governing Board. (1978). The unique role of the elementary school counselor. *Elementary School Guidance & Counseling, 12,* 200–202.

American School Counselor Association. (1979, April). Developmental guidance. *ASCA Counselor, 16,* 2–3, 11–12.

American School Counselor Association Governing Board. (1981). ASCA role statement: The practice of guidance and counseling by school counselors. *The School Counselor, 29,* 7–12.

American School Counselor Association. (1985, January). Addendum to position statement on developmental guidance. *ASCA Counselor,* p. 4.

American School Counselor Association. (1988). *Position statement: Cross/multicultural counseling.* Alexandria, VA: Author.

American School Counselor Association. (1990). *Role statement: The school counselor.* Alexandria, VA: Author.

Atkinson, D. R., Morten, G., & Sue, D. W. (1989). A minority identity development model. In D. R. Atkinson, G. Morten, & D. W. Sue (Eds.), *Counseling American minorities* (pp. 35–52). Dubuque, IA: W. C. Brown.

Axelson, J. A. (1985). *Counseling and development in a multicultural society.* Monterey, CA: Brooks/Cole.

Carey, J. C., Reinat, M., & Fontes, L. (1990). School counselors' perceptions of training needs in multicultural counseling. *Counselor Education and Supervision, 29,* 155–169.

Carter, R. T., & Helms, J. E. (1987). The relationship between black value orientations to racial identity attitudes. *Evaluation & Measurement in Counseling and Development, 19,* 185–195.

Daehler, M. W., & Bukatko, D. (1985). *Cognitive development.* New York: Random House.

Dagley, J. C. (1987). A new look at developmental guidance: The hearthstone of school counseling. *The School Counselor, 35,* 102–109.

Dinkmeyer, D. (1966). Developmental counseling in the elementary school. *Personnel and Guidance Journal, 45,* 262–266.

Elkind, D. (1984). *All grown up and no place to go: Teenagers in crisis.* Reading, MA: Addison-Wesley.

Erikson, E. H. (1950). *Childhood and society.* New York: Norton.

Erikson, E. H. (1965). *Identity: Youth and crisis.* New York: Norton.

Havighurst, R. J. (1972). *Developmental tasks and education* (3rd ed.). New York: McKay.

Hodgkinson, H. L. (1985). The changing face of tomorrow's student. *Change, 17,* 38–39.

Ibrahim, F. A., & Thompson, D. L. (1982). Preparation of secondary school counselors: A national survey. *Counselor Education and Supervision, 22,* 113–122.

Kessen, W. (1965). *The child.* New York: Wiley.

Kohlberg, L. (1966). Moral education in the schools: A developmental view. *School Review, 74,* 1–30.

Koss-Chioino, J. D., & Vargas, L. A. (1992). Through the cultural looking glass: A model for understanding culturally responsive psychotherapies. In L. A. Vargas & J. D. Koss-Chioino (Eds.), *Working with culture: Psychotherapeutic interventions with ethnic minority children and adolescents* (pp. 1–22). San Francisco, CA: Jossey-Bass.

Lee, C. C. (1989). Multicultural counseling: New directions for counseling professionals. *Virginia Counselors Journal, 17,* 3–8.

Lee, C. C. (1991). Cultural dynamics: Their importance in multicultural counseling. In C. C. Lee & B. L. Richardson (Eds.), *Multicultural issues in counseling: New approaches to diversity* (pp. 11–17). Alexandria, VA: American Association for Counseling and Development.

Mathewson, R. H. (1949). *Guidance policy and practice.* New York: Harper & Brothers.

Mead, M. (1928). *Coming of age in Samoa.* New York: Morrow.

Miller, P. (1983). *Theories of developmental psychology.* New York: W. H. Freeman.

Munroe, R. L., & Munroe, R. H. (1975). *Cross-cultural human development.* Monterey, CA: Brooks/Cole.

Muro, J. J., & Dinkmeyer, D. C. (1977). *Counseling in the elementary and middle schools.* Dubuque, IA: W. C. Brown.

Muro, J. J., & Miller, J. J. (1983). Needed: A new look at developmental guidance and counseling. *Elementary School Guidance & Counseling, 17,* 252–260.

Myrick, R. D. (1987). *Developmental guidance and counseling: A practical approach.* Minneapolis, MN: Educational Media Corp.

Myrick, R. D. (1989). Developmental guidance: Practical considerations. *Elementary School Guidance & Counseling, 24,* 14–20.

Offer, D., Ostrov, E., & Howard, K. J. (1981). *The adolescent: A psychological self-portrait.* New York: Basic Books.

Parham, T. A., & Helms, J. E. (1981). Influence of a Black student's racial identity attitudes on preference for counselor race. *Journal of Counseling Psychology, 28,* 250–257.

Phinney, J. S., & Rotheram, M. J. (Eds.). (1987). *Children's ethnic socialization: Pluralism and development.* Newbury Park, CA: Sage.

Piaget, J. (1970). *Science of education and the psychology of the child.* New York: Onion Press.

Piaget, J. (1987). *Possibility and necessity.* Minneapolis, MN: University of Minnesota Press.

Pinderhughes, C. A. (1973). Racism and psychotherapy. In C. V. Willie, B. M. Kramer, & B. S. Brown (Eds.), *Racism and mental health* (pp. 61–121). Pittsburgh, PA: University of Pittsburgh Press.

Ponterotto, J. G., & Casas, J. M. (1987). In search of multicultural competence within counselor education programs. *Journal of Counseling and Development, 65,* 430–434.

Powell, G. J., Yamamoto, J., Romero, A., & Morales, A. (Eds.). (1983). *The psychosocial development of minority group children*. New York: Brunner/ Mazel.

Rice, F. P. (1990). *The adolescent: Development, relationships, and culture* (6th. ed.). Boston: Allyn and Bacon.

Western Interstate Commission for Higher Education and the College Board. (1988). *The road to college: Educational progress by race and ethnicity*. Boulder, CO.

Wrenn, C. G. (1962). *The counselor in a changing world*. Washington, DC: American Personnel and Guidance Association.

PART II

CULTURALLY RESPONSIVE COUNSELING K-12

Counseling in the school setting is a helping process in which a counseling professional works with students, either individually or in groups, on problem solving or decision making related to academic, career, or personal/social issues. The five chapters that comprise this part of the book offer ideas on how to facilitate this process in culturally diverse school settings. These chapters focus on counseling with African American, Arab American, Asian American, Hispanic American, and Native American children and adolescents. Young people from these groups are a major part of the growing diversification of America's schools.

2

COUNSELING INTERVENTIONS WITH AFRICAN AMERICAN YOUTH

DON C. LOCKE

INTRODUCTION

There are many perspectives on how African American ethnic group membership affects the education of African American youth. In this chapter, elements of African American culture and their affect on the education of African American students will be explored. In addition, through case studies, recommendations for promoting counselor effectiveness with African American students will be offered. Finally, two secondary school counseling projects designed to enhance the education of African American students will be examined.

Many school experiences for African American students are negative due to errors of both commission and omission on the part of educational professionals. Tracking, low expectations, the absence of sufficient role models, and a disregard for cultural diversity are barriers to African American educational achievement. Berry and Asamen (1989) reported that African American children are overrepresented in the ranks of those who experience chronic school failure. This is a result of poor motivational factors such as faulty perceptions of control, low expectations for the future, and inadequate interpersonal evaluations.

African American students want to succeed academically. DeSantis, Ketterlinus, and Youniss (1990), for example, found that most African American adolescents wanted their parents to see them as academically able. In fact, these adolescents indicated that this perception by parents was more important than what friends thought about them. The implication of such a finding is that schools must (1) promote a philosophy that African American students can succeed and want to succeed, (2) commit themselves to alternative strategies for the education of African American students, and (3) inform parents of African American youth that they can have a positive influence on their child's academic orientation.

African American students should be educated within a culturally relevant framework. Racial/ethnic differences must be presented in such a manner that status as an African American is affirmed in school. It is proposed in this chapter that African American culture should serve as a foundation upon which to build and promote academic achievement for African American students.

CULTURE, AFRICAN AMERICAN STUDENTS, AND THE SCHOOL SETTING

African American youth live in two cultures—the dominant culture of the United States and one based on aspects of African ways of life that have survived in this country. A number of scholars describe these aspects of life as having African origins. Herskovits (1958), for example, identified a number of cultural elements that are carryovers from Africa and have survived among black people in the United States. These include dialect, folklore, adult-child relationships, family structure, music, generosity or hospitality, respect for the law, religion, sense of justice, and the work ethic. Holloway (1990), in discussing Africanisms in American culture, identified a number of cultural elements that came from Africa and are sustained in the United States. Among these are linguistic structure, religious practices, rituals, beliefs, music, dance, and folklore. Woodson (1968) examined African American adult-child relationships, family structure, generosity or hospitality, respect for the law, sense of justice, and work ethic. He also suggested that these concepts have their origins in Africa.

Hilliard (1976) described the core cultural characteristics of African Americans as tendencies to:

1. *Respond to things in terms of the whole picture instead of its parts.*
2. *Prefer inferential reasoning to deductive or inductive reasoning.*
3. *Approximate space, numbers, and time rather than stick to accuracy.*
4. *Prefer to focus on people and their activities rather than on things.*
5. *Tend to have a keen sense of justice and are quick to analyze and perceive injustice.*
6. *Lean toward altruism, a concern for one's fellow man.*
7. *Prefer novelty, freedom, and personal distinctiveness.*
8. *Not "word" dependent. They tend to be very proficient in nonverbal communications. (pp. 38–39)*

The challenge arises when young African Americans must incorporate into their personality aspects of the dominant culture while holding onto those traits that are derived from African/African American culture.

African American children and adolescents often encounter values in the school culture that are not consistent with the cultural socialization patterns of their family and community. Consequently, African American students may have their identity threatened since their behavior and perception of the world seem incompatible with what is expected in school. The combination of "teacher expectations, peer pressure, and the ensuing identity crisis leads to poor performance" (Berry & Asamen, 1989, p. 78).

PROMOTING COUNSELOR EFFECTIVENESS WITH AFRICAN AMERICAN STUDENTS

Differing cultural expectations affect how counselors and students relate to each other. Individual counselors must be aware of how their own cultural orientations may cause difficulties for some African American students. Counselors must avoid placing value judgments on alternative learning styles, and they must learn to distinguish between cognitive differences and mental deficiencies. Multiculturalism requires the educator to identify the different learning styles within the environment and to modify instruction accordingly. This will ensure that students with diverse learning styles will comprehend the same content.

A school counseling model proposed by Parker and McDavis (1989) has a variety of learning procedures and processes designed to fit the cultural practices and needs of African American students. The model uses a group process that enables students to express feelings, perceive a sense of belonging, and experience interpersonal learning. It also develops students' self-confidence; provides activities to gain job knowledge and develop career goals; raises students' levels of academic functioning through time management, communication skills, and empathy training; and presents activities to improve their ability to resolve personal problems. The model also helps these students understand the purpose of standardized tests and provides the opportunities to practice them.

Locke (1989) presented some guidelines for counselors to follow in order to foster the self-esteem of African American children. He suggested that counselors be open and honest in their relationships with African American children and to be open to and genuinely respect and appreciate culturally different attitudes and behaviors. Counselors should demonstrate that they value the African American culture and should seek to participate in activities in the African American community, including inviting persons from the community to the school. The counselor should eliminate all of his or her behaviors that suggest prejudice or racism. Lastly, the counselor should expect African American students to succeed.

Brooks (1985) presented some suggestions of attitudes and competencies needed by counselors of African American students: Respect the culture within the community, respect differences in people, do not limit the African American student to standard English, do not sell the standard dialect as the sole selector of the winners and the losers, and talk about the variety of American culture and languages.

Cultural inclusion for African American students might mean having schools respond in positive ways to aspects of African American culture. For example, while students are taught the value of standard English for social and economic success, the richness and validity of their cultural dialect should be appreciated. Second, African American culture would be included in the curriculum in ways that promote academic and social learning for a dual existence within the society. This would mean helping African American students gain knowledge about and appreciation for the positive aspects of their own culture, while providing opportunities for them to acquire the necessary skills for sustaining a productive life in the dominant American culture. Third, cultural inclusion would encompass cultural content and perspective in the school curriculum in ways that present a holistic view of the African and African American experience. This might include helping African American students gain an appreciation for African culture in other parts of the world (Hollins & Spencer, 1990).

Finally, a number of general recommendations are presented for more effective counseling of African American students. These recommendations are:

1. Encourage African American students to talk about themselves, their families, and their experiences to determine which strengths might be used in the process of helping them make decisions and solve problems. All of this is aimed at determining the students' belief systems. Counselors should share similar information about themselves with their African American students.
2. Counselors should ask students to describe their social class status rather than assume that the social class can be determined by observations of the student or by student behaviors.
3. Have students describe how they celebrate holidays in their family, the role of religion in their lives, and other situations in which they demonstrate pride in being African American. This information may serve as a useful springboard for group counseling sessions.
4. Have students describe their social kinship network and how it impacts their lives. This information should help the counselor understand the importance of kinship influences on student clients.
5. Feel free to give specific, explicit answers to questions raised by African American students. Remember that giving explicit advice may be perceived as a sign of genuine caring among African Americans.

6. Have African American students describe concerns about whether the counselor will be able to help them. Do not be afraid if the students articulate some ambivalence toward the counselor as a helper. This ambivalence may be because of perceived value differences, racial/ethnic group membership, or cultural differences. African American students may respond more favorably to individuals of the same race; however, they may not harbor any negative feelings toward individuals of a different race.

7. Have students articulate their concerns in their own words. It is critical that African American students be permitted and encouraged to use their everyday language to describe themselves and situations in which they are involved.

8. Connect discussions regarding behavior with individuals in their community; for example, what would (parents, guardians, members of kinship network, members of church) think about this behavior? Ask students to compare their personal views of their behavior with the views held by significant individuals in their lives.

9. Use music and dance as areas of special interest to African Americans. For example, African American students may be asked to write a "rap" to describe a particular situation, an incident, or a feeling.

10. Where possible, make visits to the homes of African American students. Counselors must be perceived as being comfortable in the environment in which their student clients live.

CASE STUDIES

The following case studies present contemporary issues confronting African American students. After each case is an analysis of the dynamics presented and specific guidelines for counselor intervention.

Denise

Denise is a 9-year-old African American girl in the fourth grade. Her elementary school is in a midsize city in the southeastern United States. Denise lives with her parents and two older brothers in an apartment complex in a working-class African American neighborhood. Because of recent redistricting, Denise is being bused from an all-black school in her neighborhood to a predominately middle-class white elementary school across town. This is her first year in the school and Denise is one of only five African American girls in the fourth grade.

Denise has always been a good student with no social problems. This had been the case when she started the year at her new school. Recently, however, Denise has gotten into fights with several of her classmates. She has also been failing to complete her classwork and has been talking back to her teacher.

The teacher suggests that the school counselor meet with Denise. She suspects that Denise might be having some problems at home that may be causing her behavior change in school.

When Denise comes to see the counselor, she appears angry and withdrawn. Before beginning to work with Denise, the counselor allows her to sit in the office and play with several educational games. It takes the counselor several sessions to get Denise to begin to talk about the problems she is having at school. Denise states that she hates the school and she hates being black. She says she wants to be like the white girls in her class, who she says are prettier, smarter, and better liked by the teacher. She also claims that many of the white children in her class make fun of her hair texture, skin color, and facial features. She says that they also tease her about living in a bad neighborhood, because it is all black. She says that when the other children pick on her, she either puts her head down on her desk and tries to ignore them or, when they make her really angry, she hits them.

Case Analysis

It is obvious that Denise has been affected by her move from an all-black school environment to a predominately white one. In her view, being white and female brings with it certain privileges within her current school setting. This perception, along with an apparent lack of cultural sensitivity and understanding on the part of her white classmates, has seriously impacted Denise's self-esteem and self-concept as an African American. This seeming attack on her ethnic identity has caused a great deal of anger and frustration for Denise, which have affected her schoolwork and her interpersonal skills.

Directions for Counseling Practice with Denise

Reviewing this case, it would seem that a culturally responsive school counseling professional would need to address the challenges associated with Denise's educational and social development with intervention at several levels.

Level 1: Denise

The first level of intervention involves direct service to Denise. In individual sessions, the counselor should work with Denise to promote her ethnic identity as an African American. It is important that the counselor explore with Denise her feelings about being an African American and her wish to be white. The counselor should validate and affirm Denise's blackness. She must be assured that her African American cultural realities are important and her physical features appreciated. Denise should be shown that being racially/ethnically different from her classmates is a positive thing.

As Denise begins to feel comfortable about her blackness, it is important that the counselor help her develop some anger management skills. These will help her to deal more effectively with interpersonal challenges involving her peers.

Another suggestion might be to get Denise and some of her African American peers involved in a group counseling experience designed to promote the development of African American identity and pride. Significantly, within a cultural context, group-oriented counseling approaches reflect the communal nature of the African American experience (Toldson & Pasteur, 1976).

A model to consider has been developed by Lee and Lindsey (1985). It is a multisession developmental group counseling experience for African American elementary school students. The group experience uses selected African American art forms (e.g., music, drama, poetry, folklore, and graphic expression) as educational aids in the counseling process. Using these art forms as a fundamental part of the group intervention, the model stresses an understanding and appreciation of African/African American culture, development of positive and responsible behavior, and modeling positive African American images.

Level 2: Denise's Classmates and Teacher

In addition to intervening with Denise, a culturally responsive counselor may need to be prepared to intervene with her peers to effect classroom change for her benefit. It appears that Denise's new school has made little allowance for cultural diversity. The white children's teasing of Denise about her racial features and her neighborhood indicates a lack of sensitivity or understanding about African American cultural realities.

In this case, a counselor should be ready to assume the role of student advocate for Denise. Acting as student advocate, the counselor should function to promote an awareness among Denise's peers about African American culture. This might include a classroom guidance experience related to African American culture and the importance of appreciating differences among people.

In addition, it may be necessary to consult with Denise's teacher to help her delineate and challenge any stereotypes she may have acquired about African American students and her expectations of them. Such consultation might include exploring ways to integrate the accomplishments of African Americans into her curriculum. This would not only bolster Denise's sense of pride but it would help the white students gain an appreciation for African American history and culture.

Jamal

Jamal is a 15-year-old African American male who is in the tenth grade at an integrated high school on the outskirts of a major city. His mother is a schoolteacher and his father is a police officer. Jamal is the oldest of four children. He is an above-average student and is in the college-preparatory track.

As part of the educational planning process for students in this track, Jamal's counselor calls him to the office to begin discussing Jamal's college plans. The counselor observes that Jamal is unusually distant and not particularly interested in his studies or going to college. This is surprising to the counselor, since Jamal is usually outgoing and appears to work hard in school. The counselor, who has had a good relationship with Jamal, inquires about what is troubling him.

Jamal says that he does not see the relevance of schoolwork to his life. He says that his courses are too "Euro-centric" and not relevant to him as an African American. He feels that being in classes that are predominately white is compromising his identity as an African American.

Jamal's circle of close friends are black males in the general-education track. These young men have been his friends since elementary school. The counselor finds out that since beginning high school, these young men have started to treat Jamal differently. They state that since he is in the college-prep track, Jamal isn't "down with the homeboys" anymore. They claim that Jamal is now acting and talking "white." According to his friends, the college-prep track is for white students and African American students who are trying to be white. As Jamal's childhood friends have started to drift away from him, he finds it difficult to develop any close friendships with his white peers. He states that he has very little in common with the white students in his classes.

The counselor consults with Jamal's parents and discovers that they, too, are concerned about his behavior. They claim that he never talks about his schoolwork anymore. They state that Jamal has told them not to tell people that he is in the college-prep track or talk about his performance in school.

Case Analysis

Jamal's case is typical of a growing phenomenon among academically successful African American students (Fordham & Ogbu, 1986). Because of peer accusations of "acting white" by getting good grades in school, many African American students are questioning the value of academic achievement. Within the peer group, achieving academically is often viewed as adopting white values and forsaking black culture. There is often tremendous pressure on hard-working African American students not to "sell out" in the eyes of their peers. This often means performing poorly in school or hiding outstanding academic achievement in an attempt to stay in favor with the peer group.

Jamal is feeling confused and alienated. His friends have communicated to him the message that somehow because he is in the college-prep track he is no longer acting black and is becoming white. He has succumbed to the prevailing value among his peers and is starting to feel that academic achievement is no longer consistent with his identity as an African American. It is obvious that peer relationships are extremely important to Jamal and that he would rather be accepted by his friends than continue to do well in school.

Directions for Counseling Practice with Jamal

It is evident that Jamal needs support to deal with the intense peer pressure he is experiencing. The counselor should be very forthright with Jamal and process his perceptions of academic achievement. He needs to understand that by achieving in school, he does not have to compromise his African American identity. The counselor should explore with Jamal the historical importance of education to African Americans. Jamal should be encouraged to attain success in school as a way to enable him to perhaps become a future leader in the ongoing struggle for African American social and economic equality. The counselor might discuss with him the fact that he has the potential to be a role model for his siblings and other young African Americans by working hard in school.

It would be important for Jamal to understand the concept of being "bicultural." The counselor should explain to him that it is important to learn to "walk the walk and talk the talk" when he is in the classroom. This does not mean that he has become white, but that he has merely learned appropriate behavior for the American macroculture. He must be led to see that when he is in African American social and communal settings, he can freely express his blackness.

To underscore the bicultural concept, the counselor might consider finding a role model for Jamal. This could be an older person, perhaps an African college student, who experienced the same type of peer pressure. It would be important for Jamal to see how an African American can succeed academically and maintain his or her ethnic identity.

If there are other African American students in the school who are experiencing similar peer pressure and alienation, the counselor might consider forming a support group. This would give Jamal and the other students the opportunity to help each other deal with the perceptions of those students who feel they are selling out or attempting to become white.

The counselor may also want to explore with Jamal the nature of friendship. They should talk about the unconditional nature of friendship and the fact that true friends are supportive no matter what an individual does. It may also be important for the counselor to consult with Jamal's parents. The counselor should stress to the parents the importance of maintaining high academic expectations, while being sensitive to the tremendous peer pressure that Jamal must confront.

FOSTERING ACADEMIC DEVELOPMENT AMONG AFRICAN AMERICAN YOUTH

Education involves nurturing the natural differences that each child brings to school. Numerous dimensions such as ability, self-confidence, emotional maturity, need for nurturing, style of learning, and facets of personality affect how students learn. Therefore, school counselors must recognize and address these natural differences.

For many African American students, radical changes are needed in educational practice to meet their needs effectively. Counselors must ensure that content from African/African American culture is included in the curriculum so that students from this ethnic background see their images in curriculum materials. Educational equity will exist when counselors and teachers become sensitive to cultural diversity and adapt their intervention styles so that they appeal to a diverse student population. To fail to do so is to waste human potential.

The following is a description of two intervention projects designed to promote the academic development of African American high school students. They serve as a model for counselors who wish to take the initiative in developing, implementing, and evaluating culturally relevant methods of addressing the educational challenges confronting African American youth.

"Getting on the Right Track"

"Getting on the Right Track" is a program developed in a North Carolina School system for African American high school students. The project was initiated as a deliberate psychological educational intervention with three objectives: (1) to make the school an effective social center for African American youth through cooperative rather than competitive learning; (2) to involve educators with the student participants as significant adults by addressing the interests of the students and acting as advocates on their behalf; and (3) to strengthen the ego identity with an Afro-centric perspective to role-taking experiences.

"Getting on the Right Track" was developed using dimensions of success proposed by Sedlacek and Brooks (1976) as the foundation for program activities. The eight dimensions suggested by Sedlacek and Brooks appear to be critical if African American students are to succeed in school. They are characteristics that seem to distinguish successful African American students from those who do not succeed in academic endeavors. The eight dimensions include:

- *Positive Self-Confidence* Students who have strong feelings of self-worth, who have strength of character, who have self-determination and independence have better chances of succeeding than those who do not.
- *Realistic Self-Appraisal* Students who have a realistic understanding of their academic strengths and weaknesses have better chances of succeeding than those who do not. When students use their strengths to work on their weaknesses, they seem to be in better positions to persevere academically and to do well in later life.
- *Understanding and Ability to Deal with Racism* African American students who understand and deal with racism effectively succeed more often than those who do not. African American students must learn how to handle prejudice and racism in ways that are not self-destructive or harmful to others.
- *Preference for Long-Range Goals Over More Immediate, Short-Term Needs* African American students who accomplish this task will succeed at a greater rate than those who must have their needs met immediately. African American history provides numerous examples of individuals who have had few of their most basic needs met and still made significant contributions to society. These role models have had a greater than ordinary ability to defer gratification.
- *Availability of a Strong Support Person* This person may be a family member, teacher, counselor, pastor, or friend. These persons help students cope, prioritize, and persevere in the face of great struggle.
- *Successful Leadership Experiences* African American students who engage in school activities and organizations have a greater likelihood of succeeding than those who participate only in classroom activities.
- *Community Service* African American students who have participated in community service have a greater chance of persevering and doing well than those who do not. Students who are

part of organizations and activities in the community that assert positively African American culture and values have an advantage over students who do not.

- *Knowledge in a Field* African American students who have knowledge acquired in a field are more likely to do well than those who do not. If students have culturally related ways of obtaining information and demonstrating knowledge, they can feel confident about the ways in which they come to new knowledge and understanding.

Ninth-grade students were selected for the project who, according to middle school personnel, were academically capable but needed some assistance in order to be able to pursue a college education after high school. Each student signed a contract that indicated a willingness to participate in all aspects of the program, including (1) commitment to pursue a college-preparatory curriculum, (2) permission of the project staff to periodically review school records, (3) adherence to a code of behavior, (4) willingness to meet regularly with a teacher-mentor and the project staff, and (5) a promise to maintain regular contact with the teacher-mentor or project counselor in case of any educational or personal problems.

Teachers volunteered to serve as mentors to students in the project. These teachers made a commitment to meet informally with project participants weekly to monitor their progress. Several mentor teachers took students for lunch on weekends, had breakfast with them at school, or spent time with them in other nonschool settings.

Parents/guardians of the participants, who are central to the success of the project, were contacted by letter and phone to inform them that their child had been selected for the project, and to request permission for their child to participate. Parents were invited to a meeting early in the school year where the project was explained to them and they were asked to sign a contract that indicated support of the project goals. By signing the contract, the parents demonstrated total commitment to the project.

Students were taken from their regular classes on a biweekly basis to participate in the project. They were instructed in African American history and culture; basic communication techniques (e.g., the importance of eye contact and assertiveness); study techniques; and strategies for successful interracial interactions. The major portion of time in these biweekly meetings was devoted to what was called an "Afro-

Centric Identity Enhancing Science Project." This is a deliberate psychological education effort suggested by Sprinthall and Scott (1989) that involves developing thinking and research skills. It included:

1. Identifying student interests and hobbies, which were translated into research questions
2. Reflecting on naming self "African American"
3. Exploring historical evidence of Africa as the "cradle of civilization"
4. Comparing the Mercator projection with the Peters projection of world maps (the Peters projection of the world shows continents in their true relative size to each other)
5. Writing letters to individuals related in some way to their research project to gain primary information
6. Preparing a research paper on their topic (topics were often related to students' regular study in science, language, or social studies)
7. Preparing an oral presentation for a science fair that was held at a local university
8. Going on a field trip to a local life and science museum (Locke & Faubert, in press).

During the second year of the project, sophomores, who had been through the experience, served as peer mentors to new freshmen who entered the program. Sophomores also directed the new freshmen in their Afro-Centric Identity Enhancing Science Project. This mentoring and teaching provided the sophomores an opportunity to participate in a significant role-taking experience (Locke & Zimmerman, 1987). Sophomores also participated in the science fair with their mentees and took a field trip to an historically black college.

The third year of the project afforded opportunity for the juniors to expand their activities, since the current sophomores assumed the roles of peer mentors for the new freshmen. Junior-year activities include researching and writing their family histories, performing some community service (e.g., volunteering at a day-care center or retirement home) for a minimum of eight hours, thoroughly investigating a minimum of five colleges/universities, participating in the regular career awareness activities at school, and a field trip to Washington, D.C.

Evaluation

The qualitative results of the project provide evidence that when school is an effective social center where cooperative learning takes place, African American students can and will succeed. They develop pride in themselves, and significant adults in their schools and communities express pleasure with their progress. Quantitative data are being collected on grades, attendance, moral development, and ego development. The primary measure of program effectiveness will be student retention in high school with a goal of 100 percent matriculation in a college or university.

"Talking in the Street and Talking in School"

"Talking in the Street and Talking in School" is a secondary school speaking skills program developed in another North Carolina school system. It was designed to dispel some misconceptions about "black English" and to help African American students become "bilingual." Because of the worth U.S. society places on language and "correct speech," black English was described in this program as useful in some settings and "standard" English useful in others. The most important message communicated to the participants was to learn the appropriate time(s) to use each. The program emphasized that students who wish to move into the mainstream of the dominant culture in the United States must have the ability to speak standard English.

Prior to the implementation of the program, students' baseline level of communication was assessed. Although this does not require the use of a speech therapist, a therapist was used in this program to determine if students were speaking black English or poor standard English. Students' speech was recorded prior to beginning the program and progress was monitored during the program and at its conclusion.

Self-concept enhancement was the first area to receive attention in the project. African American youth need to have positive feelings about themselves to be willing to attempt to speak differently in front of their peers, teachers, and other adults. Self-concept development activities included discussions about race, ethnicity, prejudice, racism, and discrimination.

The second component of the program included a focus on speech skill development in the areas of diction, rate of speech, fluency, general voice characteristics, and vocal inflection. Participants were actually taught black English so that they could know themselves when their speech was nonstandard. These areas were taught prior to beginning instruction in public speaking, the third major component of the project.

The program focused on nonverbal as well as verbal communication. Communication experts have concluded that the majority of any message is communicated nonverbally (Mehrabian, 1981). Students and teachers jointly developed culturally specific nonverbal behaviors. Students were then shown how their nonverbal messages influence their verbal ones and vice versa. Specific to the area of nonverbal communication is assertiveness and listening skills. Participants were taught how to assert themselves without being either aggressive or passive. Participants were also taught active listening skills.

Once these abilities were fairly well developed, students began developing public speaking skills by preparing speeches on topics of their choice. Students were encouraged to write speeches on topics about which they were knowledgeable. Speeches were video recorded and students were encouraged to analyze their tapes for examples of good standard English speech, as well as for their nonverbal communication.

In addition, participants explored interracial communication. They learned that they speak differently in interracial situations and discovered that their nonverbal communication differs according to racial/ethnic situations.

The final component of the project was an assessment of participant change from the initial assessment to the conclusion of the project. The final assessment included communication competence, self-reported attitudinal change, as well as reports from educators who had observed the participants in the program. This qualitative evaluation suggested that the program was a success in that participants significantly changed in their ability to speak standard English.

Since language is the foundation of all other learning, strong language development programs are important in the promotion of African American student development. African American youth must appreciate the value of being bilingual; they must understand that although it is important to value black English, they must become competent in standard English. They must see that learning standard English is essential to their future economic and social success.

Summary

Both "Getting on the Right Track" and "Talking in the Street and Talking in School" provide useful alternatives for counselors who wish to expand their service delivery to African American students. Each project was developed with the perspective that African American culture provides a viable starting point for providing effective services. The projects suggest that differential counseling services based on ethnic group membership may be needed to enhance the educational development of students whose cultural realities are often ignored in the school setting.

CONCLUSION

School counselors face major challenges in their efforts to provide effective services for all students. This chapter began with the notion that many of the experiences of African American students are negative. If school counselors are to make significant contributions to the education of African American students, they must develop an awareness of African and African American cultures. They must also understand how students are influenced by those cultures. From such awareness, counselors can develop specific strategies that address the unique needs of African American students. Such strategies were highlighted in two case studies of contemporary challenges confronting African American students. Further direction for counseling African American students was discussed in two model programs, "Getting on the Right Track" and "Talking in the Street and Talking in School." These strategies are based on the belief that knowledge is not enough; counselors must develop and execute specific programs to make contributions to the education of African American students.

REFERENCES

Berry, G. L., & Asamen, J. K. (1989). *Black students: Psychosocial issues and academic achievement.* Newbury Park, CA: Sage.

Brooks, C. K. (1985). *Tapping potential: English and language arts for the Black learner.* Urbana, IL: National Council of Teachers of English.

DeSantis, J. P., Ketterlinus, R. D., & Youniss, J. (1990). Black adolescents' concerns that they are academically able. *Merrill-Palmer Quarterly, 36,* 287–299.

Fordham, S., & Ogbu, J. U. (1986). Black students' school success: Coping with the burden of "Acting White." *Urban Review, 18,* 176–206.

Herskovits, M. J. (1958). *The myth of the Negro past.* New York: Beacon Press.

Hilliard, A. (1976). *Alternatives to IQ testing: An approach to the identification of gifted minority children.* Final report to the California State Department of Education. Sacramento, CA: Department of Education.

Hollins, E. R., & Spencer, K. (1990). Restructuring schools for cultural inclusion: Changing the schooling process for African American youngsters. *Journal of Education, 172,* 89–100.

Holloway, J. E. (1990). *Africanisms in American culture.* Bloomington: Indiana University.

Lee, C. C., & Lindsey, C. R. (1985). Black consciousness development: A group counseling model for Black elementary school students. *Elementary School Guidance & Counseling, 19,* 228–236.

Locke, D. C. (1989). Fostering the self-esteem of African-American children. *Elementary School Guidance and Counseling, 23,* 254–259.

Locke, D. C., & Faubert, M. (in press). Counselors role in deliberate psychological education. *School Counselor.*

Locke, D. C., & Zimmerman, N. (1987). Effects of peer-counseling training on psychological maturity of Black students. *Journal of College Student Personnel, 28,* 525–532.

Mehrabian, A. (1981). *Silent messages.* Belmont, CA: Wadsworth.

Parker, W. M., & McDavis, R. J. (1989). A personal development model for Black elementary school students. *Elementary School Guidance and Counseling, 23,* 244–253.

Sedlacek, W. E., & Brooks, G. C. (1976). *Racism in American education: A model for change.* Chicago: Nelson-Hall.

Sprinthall, N. S., & Scott, J. R. (1989). Promoting psychological development, math achievement, and success attribution of female students through deliberate psychological education. *Journal of Counseling Psychology, 36,* 440–446.

Toldson, I. L., & Pasteur, A. B. (1976). Therapeutic dimensions of the Black aesthetic. *Journal of Non-White Concerns in Personnel & Guidance, 4,* 195–117.

Woodson, C. G. (1968). *The African background outlined.* New York: Negro Universities Press.

ADDITIONAL RESOURCES FOR COUNSELING
WITH AFRICAN AMERICAN STUDENTS

Asante, M. K. (1987). *The Afrocentric idea.* Philadelphia, PA: Temple University.

Banks, S. L. (1985). *The education of black children and youths: A framework for educational excellence.* Columbia, MD: Fairfax.

Gill, W. (1991). *Issues in African American education.* Nashville, TN: One Horn Press.

Hale-Benson, J. E. (1986). *Black children: Their roots, culture, and learning styles.* Provo, UT: Brigham Young University Press.

Hilliard, A. G., Payton-Stewart, L., & Williams, L. O. (Eds.). (1990). *Infusion of African and African American content in the school curriculum.* Morristown, NJ: Aaron.

Jones, R. L. (Ed.). (1989). *Black adolescents.* Berkeley, CA: Cobb and Henry.

Lee, C. C. (1992). *Empowering young black males.* Ann Arbor, MI: ERIC/CAPS.

Luthuli, P. C. (1985). *What ought to be in black education.* Stoneham, MA: Butterworths.

Smith, W. D. (1989). *Black education: A quest for equity and excellence.* New Brunswick: Transaction.

3

COUNSELING YOUTH
OF ARAB ANCESTRY

MORRIS L. JACKSON

INTRODUCTION

Americans of Arab ancestry are no longer an invisible ethnic group. National and international political events have increased awareness of terms such as *Arab, Muslim,* and *Middle East* among the American public. This new awareness is evidenced by heightened curiosity about and increased questions concerning an ethnic group that has gone relatively unnoticed in U.S. society. There is now an expressed desire for information about Arab culture and Americans of Arab ancestry. In the educational system, this desire is seen in the growing interest in ways to provide more effective counseling services for children and adolescents of Arab ancestry.

The focus of this chapter is on young Americans whose cultural and ethnic origins can be traced to one of the more than 20 different countries in the Middle East and northern Africa. Arab American youth experience many of the same issues that confront all young people in American schools. However, they are also confronted with challenges such as negative stereotyping, racism and discrimination, and difficulty merging Arab culture with that of American society to create an Arab American identity. The purpose of this chapter is to provide school counselors with information to enhance their effectiveness in working with young people of Arab ancestry. The chapter is divided into two sections; the first explores specifics of Arab/Arab American culture of which school counselors should be aware when preparing to work with Arab American children and adolescents. Arab American family life, religion, and values are examined. This is followed by a discussion of important aspects of the psychosocial development of Arab American youth. Next, the chapter offers directions for culturally responsive counseling with youth of Arab ancestry and counseling case studies of Arab American students at the elementary and secondary school levels.

ARAB AMERICAN CULTURE

Any discussion of Arab American culture must consider the dynamics of family life, the significance of religion, and Arab/Arab American values. These cultural factors combine to influence the development of Arab American youth.

Family Life

Family life is an major aspect of Arab American culture. Nydell (1987) characterized this culture as a familial and kinship culture. Arab American family life can be considered from two perspectives: traditional and modern.

Traditional Arab American Family Life

The lifestyle of the traditional Arab American family consists of customs, values, beliefs, and behavioral norms that have been passed from one generation to another via an extended family network. This network stretches from the country of origin to the United States. The traditional Arab American family includes parents, grandparents, parents-in-law, children, and cousins (near and distant), regardless of their place of residence in the world (Lipson & Meleis, 1985). There is a strong sense of honor and loyalty to family in this extended kinship network. Individuals are mindful of not dishonoring the family through shameful or disgraceful acts.

Most traditional family systems have an order and structure that delineate the line of authority. In traditional Arab American families, this order and structure are patrilineal and patriarchal (Aswad, 1988;

Shabbas, 1979). Patrilineal refers to the fact that every person in the family belongs to the father's family tree and descent is traced through the male line (Shabbas, 1979). In traditional Arab American families, the father is the central authority figure. Although he may consult with his spouse regarding family matters, it is he who generally makes the final decisions. The wife/mother is generally in charge of internal affairs regarding the household, whereas the husband/father is in charge of affairs external to the home.

Modern Arab American Family Life

Through the process of acculturation, many Americans of Arab ancestry have adopted a family lifestyle similar to the traditional nuclear American family. A primary reason for this is the long absence from and disintegration of ties with countries of family origin. The modern Arab American family is generally a nuclear unit consisting of parents and children. Its members are likely to have less contact with their native country than their counterparts in a traditional family. The line of authority in a modern Arab American family is also different from that found in a traditional family. Although the father remains the central authority figure, it is not unusual for the mother to be actively involved in all the responsibilities and decisions required for the successful management of the household. The modern Arab American family adheres to a democratic and egalitarian approach to problem resolution and decision making.

Generational Differences in Arab American Family Life

Generational differences often exist in Arab American families. These differences may occur between first and second generations, second and third generations, or between first and third generations.

First-generation Arab Americans often live almost exclusively in an Arab cultural environment that they create and nurture in their local communities. Many may seek out and develop clubs, organizations, and social gatherings to reaffirm their Arab identity. The developing lifestyle affords this generation a sense of security and comfort in their new surroundings. Generally, first-generation Arab Americans build a cultural foundation on which future generations may depend for guidance and support. Therefore, the priority of this first generation is to discover how to maintain and transfer their cultural value system, cultivated in the Arab world, to their children born in the United States.

Second-generation Arab Americans often live in the cultural world their parents have created at home and the American cultural environment of the school setting and the society at large. They have a blueprint to follow about native language, behaviors, customs, and religion (Abu-Laban, 1989). This generation is thrust into the often difficult task of balancing two cultural environments. Failure to juggle these two environments successfully can lead to high levels of anxiety. Arab American young people who understand their dual role in U.S. society often face the reality of convincing their parents that they are not becoming too "American."

Conflict between generations may develop within Arab American families over definitions of appropriate behavior, male-female relations, family obligations, and respect for and obedience to elders (Abu-Laban, 1989). This is especially true if parents are determined that their children must conform exclusively to the norms of Arab culture. Arab American youth not adhering to the cultural edict of their parents are likely to experience significant levels of anxiety and stress. Non-Arabic speaking youth are more likely to be at odds with their parents' cultural system than are those who speak fluent Arabic. A loss of fluency in the Arabic language often represents movement from traditional Arab values.

Religion

An appreciation of Islam is key to understanding Arab American culture. The Arabic word *Islam* means complete submission to the will of God *(Allah)*. Islam is both a religion and a way of life. Basic to an appreciation of the faith is understanding the Articles of Faith and the Pillars of Islam. The fundamental Articles of Faith are to believe in God, His angels, His books, His messengers, and the day of judgment.

The Pillars of Islam are (1) recital of the Creed, called *Shahada* ("There is no God worthy of worship except God, and Muhammad is his messenger"); (2) prayer *(Salat)*, said five times a day—at dawn, midday, midafternoon, sunset, and nightfall; (3) paying the *Zakat* each year, which is two and a half percent of one's monies; (4) fasting during the month of Ramadan, from first light until sundown, abstaining from food, drink, and sexual relations; and (5) pilgrimage to the Holy Kaaba in Mecca once in a lifetime.

Values

Arab values are strongly influenced by Islamic traditions. Nydell (1987) identified basic values that evolve out of Islam: (1) a person's dignity, honor, and reputation are of paramount importance; (2) loyalty to one's family takes precedence over personal needs; (3) it is important to behave at all times in a manner that reflects well on others; (4) everyone believes in God and acknowledges his power; (5) humans cannot control all events—some things depend on God; and (6) piety is one of the most admirable characteristics in a person.

PSYCHOSOCIAL DEVELOPMENT OF ARAB AMERICAN YOUTH

School counseling professionals need information to help them better understand important aspects of the psychosocial development of Arab American youth. This is especially important in attempting to comprehend the cultural and ethnic identity of Arab American young people. This identity is a product of interaction with the family, the Christian or Muslim Arab American community, and mainstream American culture. These interactions can lead to one of three identities, which Arab American youth may adopt as their perceived self: Arab, Arab American, or American. School counselors should attempt to understand the identity preference of young people of Arab ancestry in order to maximize their effectiveness in the counseling relationship.

Meleis (1982) has defined an Arab as a person who speaks Arabic and shares values and beliefs of the Arabic culture. A more inclusive definition of an Arab offered by Gray and Ahmed (1988) is that an Arab is a person who considers himself or herself a member of the Arab "nation," enjoying a common heritage, language, and culture, and sharing a common destiny. However, many youth of Arab ancestry in the United States do not identify with the Arabic culture. This may be particularly true in parts of the country where there are small populations of Arab ancestry. In sparsely populated Arab American communities, there is likely to be an absence of the religious and social institutions needed to provide the foundation support and guidance required for the development of an Arab identity.

Throughout their development, however, Arab American young people are often responded to by Anglo Americans as if they were an Arab first and an American second. This is especially true when there are unfavorable political events involving the United States and one of the Arab-speaking countries of the world. Second-, third-, and fourth-generation Arab Americans born in the United States are still subjected to unkind words and comments because of the often negative emphasis placed on cultural differences in the United States.

Young people from Arab backgrounds may forge an Arab American identity as a way of coping with the daily anxiety created by the conflict of cultural values. An Arab American identity represents a compromise in cultures. One of the developmental tasks for young Arab Americans is navigating their way through both the Arab and American cultures.

DIRECTIONS FOR CULTURALLY RESPONSIVE COUNSELING WITH YOUTH OF ARAB ANCESTRY

The growing presence of students of Arab ancestry in America's schools presents opportunities for school counseling professionals to examine their effectiveness in working with this client group. School counselors must look beyond traditional intervention approaches and identify strategies that may be culturally responsive in addressing the educational needs of Arab American young people. Counselors wishing to maximize their effectiveness with this diverse student population need a repertoire of culturally responsive skills. The following represent some directions for culturally responsive counseling with Arab American youth. Such counseling intervention can take place at the individual, group, or systemic level.

Appreciate the Importance of Family

It is important to note that Arab American youth in the process of acculturation into American society, as a rule, are not likely to seek counseling outside the family. Within traditional Arab society, family members seeking counseling from strangers would be viewed with shame and disdain. Family influences are so important that they not only provide emotional support but may also play a role in academic and career decision making (Al-Ahmady, 1988). Therefore, counselors attempting to counsel a student of Arab ancestry regarding academic or career choice should actively consider the recommendations of parents prior to offering guidance to the student.

It is important for school counselors to know if Arab American students are a product of a modern or traditional family. The father is the most appropriate family member to consult with about family composition and whether traditional Arab values are emphasized in the home.

Understand the Level of Acculturation

An Arab American student's acculturation into the American mainstream directly relates to the number of U.S. values he or she has adopted. Each American value that an Arab American student adopts may distance him or her further from traditional Arab culture. Some factors that school counselors may need to consider in determining the level of acculturation among Arab American youth are (1) the ability to speak and understand Arabic versus command of the English language, (2) being born and raised in the United States versus immigrating to the United States at a young age, (3) acceptance versus rejection of Arabic values, (4) having one's first name Americanized (e.g., *Joe* Saeed), and (5) extensive contact with nonfamily members and nonethnic community members.

An Arab American student who has achieved a high degree of acculturation into mainstream American society is most likely to seek out a counselor for a range of issues and concerns. These concerns may be consistent with the problems that any student may have in the school setting. The counselor who collects family background information on such a student is apt to learn that he or she is probably a member of a modern Arab American family system. Such knowledge could help in deciding the degree to which the head of the family should be involved in the counseling process. With this student group, however, it is a good idea to consider informing the parents about counseling sessions with their children and the topics that will be discussed.

Consider the Importance of Religion

Counselors should be acutely aware of the religious preference of their Arab American students. This can provide valuable insight into the acculturation of a student into mainstream American culture. This information can also assist school counselors in establishing rapport with Arab American students. Rapport building can be enhanced if the counselor knows whether a student is a Christian or a Muslim. A student who is of the Christian faith is likely to have more in common with a counselor than one who is a Muslim. Counselors may have to work harder to establish rapport with a Muslim student.

Consider the Impact of Sex-Role Socialization

Jackson (1991) suggested that cross-sex counseling with Arab Americans should be considered with caution, given Arab cultural traditions about segregation of the sexes. Therefore, counselors may need to refer an Arab American student to a same-sex counselor whenever necessary. A student of Arab ancestry is likely to be more comfortable and more responsive with a same-sex counselor. Also, rapport and trust are more readily established in same-sex counseling interactions, which may lead to elimination of barriers in the helping relationship.

Move Beyond Stereotypes

Stereotyping of Arab American youth can interfere with the counseling relationship. Communication barriers are likely to occur if the counselor harbors stereotypical assumptions about a student of Arab ancestry. Resistance and lack of trust are examples of communication barriers noted to be problematic in the counseling relationship with Arab American clients (Jackson, 1991). School counselors need to ensure that their conscious and unconscious stereotypes about people of Arab ancestry do not impede their therapeutic relationship with Arab American youth. They should determine the cultural and ethnic preference of these young people and recognize and accept the diversity of Arab Americans.

Employ Group Interventions

An intervention strategy that is consistent with Arab culture is to offer group counseling programs for Arab American students on issues of mutual interest or concern. Group counseling would be an activity that reflects the Arab value of collectivism. In deference to Arabic custom and Islamic tradition, it might be important to ensure that members of a group are all of the same sex.

Consider Counseling Style

Counselors may need to study closely elements implicit in their counseling style that may conflict with the value system of Arab American youth. For example, counselors may need to be mindful of their nonverbal messages, such as eye contact, tone of voice, rate of speech, loudness, and physical distance from another person (Barouki & Winter, 1990). For example, Hall (1979) suggested that people of Middle-Eastern origin maintain a conversational distance of two feet in comparison to five feet for Americans.

In counseling Arab Americans, Abudabbeh (1991) suggested that cognitive therapy may be the most useful intervention because of reluctance on the part of this cultural group to express feelings to strangers. Abudabbeh also pointed out that Arabs consider it impolite and shameful to use the first person pronoun *I* in the therapeutic relationship. This suggests that counselors should maintain a professional dialogue throughout the counseling session. For example, instead of saying, "I think...," the counselor may say, "It is my professional judgment that...." This will allow the counselor to keep the respect of the client in the counseling session.

Employ Systemic Intervention

Counselors should play a facilitative role in heightening the awareness of the total school environment about possible value differences and areas of conflict between American and Arab culture. Acting as consultants, counselors could organize planning meetings with groups of educational professionals and students to brainstorm ideas to effectively meet the academic and social needs of Arab American youth. An important outcome of these planning meetings should be heightened awareness of Arab American culture and the kind of issues impacting on the psychosocial development of Arab American youth. In addition, the counseling staff might consider organizing workshops for school personnel, perhaps with an expert on Arabic culture, to enhance the understanding of Arab/Arab American student culture and behavior. A list of resources on Middle Eastern culture is included at the end of this chapter.

CASE STUDIES

Farida

Farida is a 7-year-old Jordanian American girl. She is in the second grade and attends a public elementary school located in a suburban neighborhood. There are approximately 825 students enrolled at her school, the majority of whom are European American. Children from ethnic minority groups comprise about 10 percent of the student population. There are only five students of Arab ancestry attending the school.

Farida was born in Jordan and immigrated to the United States with her parents at the age of 5. She has attended school in the United States for two years. At the time of her arrival, Farida was able to communicate quite well with her parents in Arabic. Her command of the English language has been evaluated as fair. She prefers to talk with her parents in Arabic—in spite of the fact that her parents insist that she use English in order to receive as much practice in that language as possible.

Farida's parents immigrated to the United States for economic advancement and to seek better educational opportunities for their children. Her parents, as first-generation Arab Americans, emphasize the importance of maintaining traditional Arab values. There are no extended family members living in their home and both parents are employed full time. The parents' religious preference is Muslim and they are raising their children in that faith. They are also actively involved in the Muslim Arab American community. Through this community, Farida has friends of Arab ancestry with whom she socializes and speaks her native language. However, Farida also has American friends in her neighborhood with whom she plays.

Farida was referred to the school counselor by her teacher. The teacher noticed that Farida is not fully participating in classroom activities and that her grades are beginning to decline. The teacher also reported that during free play time, Farida is reluctant to interact with her classmates. In addition, the other students in the class tease her and call her names.

Case Analysis

Farida appears to have difficulty with her communication skills because of her lack of mastery and fluency in the English language. Second, she appears to have some difficulty in adjusting to the new cultural environment—despite the fact that she has lived in the United States for two years. She appears to have a conflict between U.S. and Arabic values. American values are encouraged in the school and Arabic values are reinforced at home. The teasing and name calling from the other students may be related to cultural misunderstanding.

Recommended Counselor Action

The following course of action is suggested in Farida's case. First, the counselor should contact Farida's parents and invite them for a conference. At this conference, the counselor should explain his or her role, since this may be the first time that the family has been involved with the counseling process. The counselor should explain Farida's difficulties and discuss strategies for addressing them. It is important that the counselor obtain the approval of Farida's parents before attempting to implement the strategies.

During the conference, the counselor should explain the difficulty Farida is having balancing American and Arabic values. The counselor should explore with her parents which value system is most important to them, so that system may be reinforced in working with Farida.

Second, the counselor should make attempts to enroll Farida in an English as a Second Language program to increase her mastery of English and improve her communication skills. If the school does not have such a program, the counselor should identify one in the community.

Third, the counselor should consult with Farida's teacher to suggest that she be paired with a native-born American student who could help her by conversing in English with her. Farida's cultural adjustment could be greatly assisted through this pairing.

Fourth, the counselor might coordinate guidance activities with Farida's class. The focus of these activities should be on helping the children develop an understanding of themselves and people who come from different cultural backgrounds.

Hind

Hind is a 13-year-old girl in the eighth grade at an urban junior high school. Students attending the school represent various cultural and ethnic groups. Even though the school was considered to have one of the most diverse student populations in the city, the majority of the students enrolled there are European American. Hind is the only student of Arab ancestry at the school.

Hind was born in the United States, where she has spent all her school years. She is an excellent student and has a grade-point average of A- in all her academic courses. She is fluent in English and has partial command of the Arabic language. She understands the Arabic spoken by her parents, but is not able to converse with them in that language. At home, her parents insist that she attempt to speak Arabic as much as possible.

The majority of Hind's friends at school are European American. However, her circle of friends outside of school consists mainly of Arab Americans. This is partly because of the socialization by her parents who involve her in social activities with other families of Arab ancestry.

Hind's parents were born in Iraq and have lived in the United States for 16 years. Her father completed his doctoral studies at an American university. Her parents are Muslim and strongly encourage Hind to practice Islam. They are actively involved in a mosque and Hind is expected to worship with them. Her parents are employed full time and both are actively involved in Hind's schooling.

Hind was referred to the school counselor by several of her teachers who were concerned because she seemed depressed and not focused on her studies. She explained to the counselor that there were several school functions and activities in which she wished to participate, such as a school dance and cheerleading. However, her parents denied her permission to participate. In addition, she had requested permission from her parents to attend the movies with several female and male friends, but they had adamantly denied her request. Hind expressed frustration about being unable to participate in what she considered normal activities for girls her age. This was difficult for Hind to discuss with her parents and she was reluctant to openly share her frustration with them. Although she had discussed her concerns with some of her female classmates, they did not seem to fully understand her frustrations.

Case Analysis

It seems reasonable to assume that Hind is having difficulty determining what is acceptable and appropriate behavior for herself within the context of cultural expectations. Specifically, she appears to be struggling with acceptable American behavior as opposed to acceptable behavior in the Arab religious and cultural tradition. It is evident that Hind's parents have attempted to instill in her Arab values. On the other hand, she wishes to adopt the behavior and attitudes of U.S. adolescent culture. Hind appears to be trying to resolve her identity as both an American and an Arab.

Recommended Counselor Action

Throughout the counseling process, the counselor should be guided by an awareness of what is considered proper female behavior in Arab culture and the strong influence that parents, particularly fathers, have in socializing young people. Therefore, it is first advisable for the counselor to talk with Hind and get her perspective on her problem. The two of them should jointly explore possible alternatives for solving Hind's perceived problem—namely, how she can be a "typical" American teenager and still respect her parent's cultural expectations.

Next, the counselor should obtain permission from Hind to consult with her parents. When the parents come to see the counselor, it may be important to discuss with them Hind's cultural dilemma. The goal should be to help the parents understand the scope of Hind's depression. It might be helpful to invite the parents, particularly Hind's father, to explain proper female adolescent behavior within their cultural context. The counselor should then attempt to explain the typical developmental dynamics of adolescence in American culture. Together, the counselor and Hind's parents might explore ways to help Hind bridge the cultural chasm—specifically, to find possible areas of compromise that will allow Hind to participate in American age-appropriate activities while maintaining her ties to Arab culture.

After meeting with the parents, the counselor should conduct a session with Hind and her parents. The counselor should be available as a resource person as Hind and her parents discuss ways to address the issues that confront her.

George

George is a 17-year-old American of Arab ancestry who was born in a rural town in the Northwest. He is in the eleventh grade. George is fluent in English and is not able to speak, read, or understand Arabic. He is an average student who is actively involved in sports, especially football. He has to work hard to maintain a C average in order to maintain his athletic eligibility.

George is a product of a cross-cultural marriage. His mother is European American and his father is an Egyptian American, who immigrated to the United States 20 years ago. George's parents divorced when he was 7 years old. His mother retained custody of George and continues to raise him. Prior to the divorce, George's father indicated that he wanted to instill Arabic values in his son. However, the divorce made it nearly impossible for his father to continue to influence George in the manner he desired. However, his father maintains telephone contact with his son and visits him twice yearly.

The majority of George's friends are European American and he perceives himself to be an American. He states that at no time has he ever considered himself to be Egyptian American. It should be noted that George's family name is the same as his father's, which could identify him as a person of Arab ancestry. The only time George comes in contact with Arabic people is when he visits his father. George states that he never discusses his cultural heritage with his peers. Consequently, none of his friends know that his father's ethnic background is Egyptian.

George impresses one as an average American student. He regularly attends a Catholic church with his mother and seems to possess the cultural values of a typical American teenager.

George was referred to the school counselor by the football coach. George had recently visited the coach's office to discuss a problem that was developing with members of the football team. He told the coach he was "mad as hell" and was contemplating quitting the team. It seems that some of the players were calling him names such as "terrorist," "camel lover," and a "dirty fundamentalist." Because of this, George had become involved in a fight in the locker room. Some of the players on the team said they did not understand why he had such an odd-sounding last name. The deterioration in relationships between George and some of the football players began during the Persian Gulf War. Some students began to characterize George as an Arab who sympathized with Iraq. In the process of verbally defending himself, George had revealed that his father was Egyptian. The students assumed all Arabs and Arab Americans supported Iraq in the war.

Case Analysis

Issues of identity and stereotypical views seem to be the key concerns in this case. George seems to have been subjected to stereotypical comments implying that all Arabs and Americans of Arab descent are alike. Prior to this situation, George was accepted among his peers as an American. He perceived himself to be an American, but world events brought to surface the fact that he was an American of Egyptian ancestry. This was compounded by his peers stereotyping him and not recognizing him as an individual.

Recommended Counselor Action

The counselor should meet with George and discuss his feelings of anger. In discussing these feelings, he should be afforded the opportunity to examine issues of his cultural identity. The counselor should help George to process and clarify his feelings about his mixed cultural heritage. It might be important to help George explore his Arab heritage to gain a greater appreciation of that part of his identity. The counselor might wish to consult with George's father in this process.

In addition, it is important that the counselor address stereotypical views about Arab culture that exist in the school setting. The counselor might design an awareness program focusing on exploring various cultures in the United States. Arab culture should be emphasized in such a program.

CONCLUSION

The emergence of Americans of Arab ancestry as a viable cultural group contributes significantly to the growing cultural diversity of the United States. As young people from this cultural background enter the nation's schools in ever-increasing numbers, it is important that educators are equipped to meet their developmental needs. This chapter has attempted to provide school counseling professionals with information necessary to deliver quality services to Arab American youth. It is hoped that counselors will go beyond the information provided in this chapter to broaden their understanding of Arab culture, particularly key aspects of Muslim/Islamic tradition. Such an effort will increase their effectiveness with Arab American youth.

REFERENCES

Abdudabbeh, N. (1991, April). Cultural differences should be considered in treating Arab-Americans. Interview conducted by Rojean Wagner. *Psychiatric Times: Medicine & Behavior, 8,* (4), 15–17.

Abu-Laban, S. M. (1989). Arab-Canadian family life. *Arab Studies Quarterly,* 2, 135–156.

Al-Ahmady, M. E. (1988). *The importance of various guidance and counseling functions at King Abdul Aziz University, Saudi Arabia as perceived by administrators, faculty, and students.* Doctoral Dissertation, Ohio University.

Aswad, B. C. (1988). Strength of the Arab family for mental health considerations and therapy. In N. A. Gray & I. Ahmed (Eds.), *The Arab-American family: A resource manual for human service providers* (pp. 93–97). Detroit, MI: Arab Community Center for Economic and Social Socials.

Barouki, A. S., & Winter, W. D. (1990). *Serving the mental health needs of Arab-Americans.* Paper presented at the Second Annual Conference on Cultural Conflict and Trauma. Sponsored by Naim Foundation for Health-Social Care and Center for Contemporary Arab Studies, Georgetown University, Washington, DC.

Gray, N. A., & Ahmed, I. (1988). *The Arab-American family: A resource manual for human service providers.* Dearborn, MI: Arab Community Center for Economic and Social Services.

Hall, E. T. (1979). Learning the Arabs' silent language. Interview conducted by K. Friedman. *Psychology Today, 8,* 45-54.

Jackson, M. L. (1991). Counseling Arab-Americans. In C. C. Lee & B. L. Richardson (Eds.), *Multicultural issues in counseling: New approaches to diversity.* Alexandria, VA: American Association for Counseling and Development.

Lipson, J. G., & Meleis, A. I. (1985). Culturally appropriate care: The case of immigrants. *Topics in Clinical Nursing, 7,* 48-56.

Meleis, A. I. (1982). Arab students in Western universities: Social properties and dilemmas. *Journal of Higher Education, 53* (4), 439–447.

Meleis, A. I., LaFevre, C. W. (1984). The Arab-American and psychiatric care. *Perspectives in Psychiatric Care, 22,* 72–76.

Nydell, M. (1987). *Understanding Arabs: A guide for westerners.* Yarmouth, ME: Intercultural Press.

ADDITIONAL RESOURCES FOR COUNSELING WITH STUDENTS OF ARAB ANCESTRY

Films and Video

A common ground: Where three religions come together. (1987). Washington, DC: Middle East Institute.

Arab world almanac. (1991). Washington, DC: AmidEast, Inc.

Introduction to the Arab world. (1989). Washington, DC: AmidEast, Inc.

The Arabs in America. (1981). Washington, DC: AmidEast, Inc.

Books

Grabhorn-Friday, A., & Staab, R. L. (Eds.). (1991). *A resource guide to the Middle East.* Tucson, AZ: Middle East Studies Association, University of Arizona.

Haddad, Y. (1987). *Islamic values in the United States: A comparative study.* New York: Oxford University Press.

Shabbas, A. (1987). *Resource guide to materials on the Arab world.* Berkeley, CA: Arab World and Islamic Resources and School Services.

Shabbas, A., & Al-Qazzaz (1990). *The Arab world notebook: Secondary school level.* Berkeley, CA: Arab World and Islamic Resources and School Services.

Shabbas, A., El-Shaieb, C., & Nabusi, A. (1991). *The Arabs: Activities for the elementary school level.* Berkeley, CA: Arab World and Islamic Resorces and School Services.

Valente, R. A., & Newnam, C. (Eds.). (1991). *A curriculum resource guide on the Middle East.* New York: Middle East Studies Program, Forham Univesity.

MIDDLE EAST OUTREACH PROGRAM

Boston University
African Studies Center
270 Bay State Road
Boston, MA 02215
(617) 353-7303
ATTN: Jo Anne Sullivan

Columbia University
Middle East Institute
420 West 118th Street
New York, NY 10027
(212) 280-3525, 2584
ATTN: Lisa Anderson

Duke University
Islamic & Arabian Development
Studies Program
2114 Campus Drive
Durham, NC 27706
(919) 684-2446
ATTN: Bruce Lawrence

Fordham University
Middle East Studies Program
113 West 60th Street
New York, NY 10023-7475
(212) 636-6390, 6389
ATTN: Ralph Valente

Georgetown University
Community Resource Center
Center for Contemporary Arab
Studies
501 Intercultural Center
Washington, DC 20057
(202) 687-5793
ATTN: Nina Dodge

Hartford Seminary
Duncan Black Macdonald Center
for the Study of Islam and
Christian-Muslim Relations
77 Sherman Street
Hartford, CT 06105
(203) 232-4451
ATTN: Elizabeth D'Amico

Harvard University
Teaching Resource Center
Center for Middle East Studies
1737 Cambridge Street
Cambridge, MA 02138
(617) 495-4078, 7940
ATTN: Carol Shed

**New York and Princeton
Universities**
Joint Center for Near Eastern
Studies
c/o Hagop Kevorkian Center
New York University
50 Washington Square South
New York, NY 10003
(212) 998-8877 (NYU)
(609) 452-4272 (Princeton)
ATTN: Shelby Allen (NYU)
ATTN: Jerry Clinton (Princeton)

Ohio State University
Middle East Program
308 Dulles Hall
230 West 17th Avenue
Columbus, OH 43210-1367
(614) 422-9660
ATTN: Alan Payind

Asian/Asian American culture places great importance on group orientation rather than individual action. This orientation stresses that family needs take precedence over individual independence. The importance of the family, obedience to its authority, and respect for elders define key aspects of the self-concept. Personal behavior reflects not only on the individual but on one's entire family. Pride and shame, for example, are reflections on one's family rather than on one's self.

Harmonious interpersonal relationships are highly valued among most of the ethnic groups that comprise Asian/Asian American culture. To maintain these relationships, a restrained orientation is assumed in most interactions. Confrontive, directive, or harsh behavior is generally to be avoided.

CULTURE AND THE PSYCHOSOCIAL DEVELOPMENT OF ASIAN AMERICAN YOUTH

Asian/Asian American culture can have an effect on the psychosocial development of Asian American youth. The extent of this effect is often dependent on the degree of acculturation experienced by a young person and his or her family. Despite the effects of acculturation, however, a school counseling professional should have an understanding of some important dimensions in the identity development of young people of Asian ancestry.

Asian American children may derive from family traditions a conservative identity characterized by interpersonal reserve and restraint. Obeying parents and the honor of family are of paramount importance, shaping attitudes, values, and behavior. Young people are often socialized from an early age that the needs of one's family come before one's own desires. Hard work and achievement in education are also highly valued in Asian cultural traditions. This expectation can often involve a young person in long hours of studying and strenuous academic work to achieve high grades in school. Academic achievement is seen as reflecting on the honor of the family.

Acculturation is a major variable that impacts aspects of Asian/Asian American culture and affects the psychosocial development of Asian American youth. Asian American young people differ in the degree to which they become acculturated. In many instances, it may be dependent on the rate of acculturation of the family. For the Asian American adolescent, it may also be influenced by peer acceptance and pressure.

As acculturation occurs, cultural conflict may become a reality for many Asian American youth. Socialized in a highly collectivistic culture where individual identity is often indistinguishable from family identity, many young people experience anxiety, confusion, and stress when exposed to the value of individuality characteristic to the predominant American culture. Exposed to the notion of personal choice in U.S. society, many Asian American youth find it difficult to reconcile filial piety with individual goals (Lee & Cynn, 1991; Sue & Sue, 1991). Significantly, many of the psychosocial issues that confront school counseling professionals in working with Asian American students focus on the stress of meeting parental obligations while striving for individuality.

IMPORTANT CONSIDERATIONS IN THE ASIAN AMERICAN EDUCATIONAL EXPERIENCE

Asian American students often bear the burden of the "model minority" myth. This myth evokes images of a supernormal group that is overwhelmingly successful academically (Suzuki, 1990). Izawa (1988), however, debunked this myth, stating that not all Asian American students excel academically. There are many average and below-average Asian American students. In addition, they contribute to the nation's dropout rate (Rong & Preissle-Goetz, 1990). More often than not, these are the Asian American students who are overlooked and in need of counseling services.

Sue and Sue (1990) have insisted that the model minority myth must be dispelled. As long as it is perpetuated, Asian Americans will be shortchanged in terms of overall educational development. Suzuki (1990) emphasized that as long as the model minority myth defines the school experience for Asian American students, the actual facts and issues related to their overall educational needs will be ignored.

As stated earlier, Asian American students come from a culture that places great value on education. Educational achievement is paramount for young people and academic success is related to family honor. Because of this, young people often have great academic expectations imposed on them by parents. In addition, because of the model minority myth, great expectations may also be imposed on them by school and society. Asian American students are often under tremendous pressure to succeed at high academic levels. These expectations and the resulting pressure can place Asian American youth under significant amounts of stress.

In addition to academic expectations, many Asian American parents often have established specific career goals for their children. Despite achievement in academic fields related to a preordained career, Asian American students may find little fulfillment in their studies and minimal interest in a family-designated career choice. The traditions of filial piety, however, often make it difficult or impossible for students to express dissatisfaction with a career choice or to make an independent choice with respect to the world of work.

COUNSELING ASIAN AMERICAN STUDENTS: A FOCUS ON KOREAN AMERICANS

Introduction

The majority of Korean Americans immigrated to the United States following the Immigration Act of 1965. Since then, they have rapidly increased in number, averaging annually at about 33,000 new immigrants to the country (Yu, 1990). The 1990 census estimated a total of 798,849 Korean Americans living in the country, with 33 percent of the total residing in the state of California.

Although Korean American youth share cultural values and traditions similar to other Asian Americans, they must be viewed separately in light of their recent immigration history. A majority of Koreans are recent immigrants who have lived in the country for less than a decade. As a result, Korean American youth are often caught between their traditional culture and that of mainstream U.S. society as they struggle to define their identity. This cultural conflict often triggers a wide range of self-defeating and self-destructive behaviors. The cultural conflict and the trauma of immigration may place many Korean American children and youth at risk of emotional and behavioral problems that may ultimately lead to academic failure, truancy, and gang involvement in the schools.

This section of the chapter attempts to highlight the psychosocial issues in cultural adjustment for Korean American youth with an emphasis on parent/child conflict. Moreover, practical counseling techniques and strategies for school counselors are provided for the prevention of adjustment related difficulties among Korean American youth and families.

Parent/Child Conflict

Cultural conflict between parents and children is perhaps the main reason for a wide range of adjustment-related difficulties among Korean American students. A majority of Korean American parents are recent immigrants with little or no knowledge of the English language. Many are isolated from U.S. society due to language difference and opposing cultural values. As children struggle to adapt and fit into the dominant American culture, parents are fighting to keep Korean cultural traditions and values alive in their children. As this cultural gap grows wider, parents become frustrated and, out of desperation, often resort to severe forms of corporal punishment and unrealistic demands. In the process, children are pushed further and further away from their parents and the traditional value system.

Educational Values

Korean values, traditions, and social structure are strongly influenced by Confucian ideology that places great importance on hierarchical relations, respect for authority, and education. Providing a good education for their children is the most common reason stated by Korean parents for immigrating to the United States. Such a high value is placed on education that many Korean American students are under intense pressure to succeed in school at all costs. They are driven and controlled by parental pressure and guilt to attain academic excellence. Their expectations are often unrealistic and the children's inability to perform creates desperation and achievement anxiety (Lee & Cynn, 1991). It is not uncommon, for example, to find first-graders with pre-ulcer conditions due to high anxiety and pressure to be at the top of their class.

Many young people are unable to verbalize their anxiety and tend to cry out for help through physical symptoms and complaints, such as sleeplessness, loss of appetite, and stomach pains. Many adolescents who are in serious conflict with their parents tend to display their frustration and anger in more destructive ways, such as drinking, engaging in illegal activities (e.g., auto theft, robbery, and assault), failing classes, and dropping out of school. In addition, there are those who suffer silently—the so-called model minority who behaves well and attains straight As in school. They are in constant competition with others and often are their own worst enemy. Suicidal ideation is common among such success-driven students who cannot bear to lose and feel completely worthless at the slightest academic setback.

Parents instill educational values at a early age, often to the point of "brainwashing" their children that in order to be successful in this country and be treated with respect, academic excellence is paramount. Young people often grow up feeling inadequate and suffer from low self-esteem because they are not able to meet these expectations. They are easily discouraged and many express feelings of failure and a limited future because of poor school performance. It should be pointed out that even if the students are doing well, it is still perceived as inadequate by self and parents. This all-or-nothing mentality is often the outcome of parental messages and the means used to encourage children to succeed.

Social Life

Given the importance placed on education, many Korean American parents do not understand their children's desire to participate in social activities outside the classroom. Such activities are viewed as distractions that interfere with school work. Dating, going to parties, and athletic events, which are considered an integral part of the adolescent years and school life in the United States, may be viewed as corruptive in the minds of many Korean American parents. In Korea, students spend their entire time in school, concentrating solely on academic work and preparing for college examinations. Extracurricular activities and the freedom that often accompany them are nonexistent in Korea until the college years.

In the minds of many Korean American students who are struggling to be a part of the mainstream culture and be accepted by their peers, parental views about social activities are considered unreasonable. However, many young people will not openly defy their parents out of fear and an obligation to be obedient and respectful. They often engage in these activities secretly (e.g., putting on makeup in the school bathroom, sneaking out to parties and dates, getting involved in sports or clubs, and pretending to study after school). Not surprisingly, many Korean students lead double lives—speaking Korean, being obedient, dependent, and studious at home, and speaking English, and struggling to be independent, outspoken, and assertive at school.

Often, parents are unaware of their children's involvement in social activities outside the home. In addition to children's attempts to hide their social lives, parents often do not have the time to supervise or spend time with their children. Typically, both father and mother work full time, often until late in the evening and even on weekends. According to Yu (1987), these overworked parents simply do not have the time to provide emotional, social, and educational support. Many take little interest in the developmental and mental health needs of their children as long as they are bringing home good grades. Therefore, it comes as a surprise to many parents when they discover that their son or daughter dates, has problems at school, abuses drugs, and/or is involved in delinquent activities.

Communication Styles/Barriers

Traditional Practice
For centuries, open communication between Korean children and their parents has been rare or nonexistent. The hierarchical relationship between parents and children dictates that children must listen and not question the authority of their parents, especially the father. Any expression of thoughts or feelings is considered arrogant and defiant and the child is immediately reprimanded. Typically, children sit with their eyes on the floor and silently listen to their parents. They are very seldom encouraged to share their thoughts or feelings. Understandably, the tendency for Korean American students to be passive and silent in school is due primarily to their early training by parents to respect and obey authority figures.

This is not to assume, however, that all Korean American youth are obedient and passive in front of their parents. Many have violated this cultural norm as family values and structure fall apart amidst the pressures from the dominant American society. For many young people, years of pent-up frustration and anger have broken their silence. Many Korean American probationers and juvenile delinquents who are forced to receive mental health services share feelings of built-up frustration and strong desire to break away from the family. Statements such as "I can't take it anymore" or "I'm not going to just sit there and do what they say" are common. They have become frustrated, especially with their fathers, who are authoritarian and controlling. However, once the code of honor and respect is broken in the home, fathers often refuse to understand or forgive their children, who they feel have brought shame and disrespect to the family. When it becomes unbearable to stay at home, many Korean American youth often resort to running away or self-abusive behaviors to escape their family reality.

Internalized Messages

Many Korean American young people grow up feeling unloved by parents who often send threatening messages to their children as a method of discipline. "Don't even think about coming home if you get another C on your report card," or "I can't believe you are actually my son/daughter. You are a disgrace and embarrassment to all of us," or "I am going to get old quickly and die because of you" are the types of parental messages frequently heard by many Korean American youth. Children internalize these messages and begin to believe that they are a failure and unworthy of parental love. In addition to psychological and emotional changes that affect all adolescents, Korean American youth have to grapple with language difference, cultural confusion, and minority status (Yu, 1987). They often lack parental support, encouragement, and understanding at a time when it is most needed. Parents' main concern is on their children's school performance rather than on issues related to adjustment that impact their overall well-being.

Parents often set expectations for their children without taking into account their capabilities. Consequently, parental expectations and reality usually do not coincide. Parents then become disappointed and upset. There is also a strong work ethic among Koreans. If their children are not performing, many parents believe that it is due to their lack of effort. Parents' use of such harsh and conditional language is mainly out of disappointment and anger that their children did not make the needed effort to meet their expectations.

However, parents do so without understanding the damaging implications to children's self-esteem and mental health.

Comparison

Among many parents, there is a frequent tendency to compare their children with others who are doing well in school or are successful. "So and so is going to Harvard; why can't you?" or "I heard that even so and so got As in all his classes; why can't you do it?" or "Your brother/sister listens and behaves so well in school; can't you be more like him/her?" Parents use constant comparisons with others, not to intentionally insult or undermine their children, but to display their frustration that others are doing better than their children. It is also to remind them that "If they can do it, so can you."

Typically, children's academic and career success are regarded as a reflection of good parenting and high status among Korean Americans. Degrees, names of the school, types of occupation, and wealth are all indicators of success. As a result, parents push their children from a very early age to excel in school and become doctors and lawyers. This will ensure not only a bright future for their children but also gain community respect for the parents. Although it is most parents' intention to encourage and enable their children, young people often resent being compared to others, because it reinforces their feelings of inadequacy and contributes to low self-esteem.

Expression of Love

Many Korean children grow up never hearing the actual words *I love you* from their parents. This is not to say that Korean parents do not love their children. Parental love and affection is expressed in other ways, such as providing physical nourishment and comfort. Moreover, it is expressed through the sacrifice inherent in immigrating to the United States and working long hours to ensure a good education and a promising future.

Children, however, have difficulty translating such actions and sacrifice as parental love. They are heavily influenced by American media that often portray families that openly communicate and express love and affection for one another. Many Korean American youth feel rejected and resentful of their parents who are not perceived as affectionate and seldom initiate dialogue outside of school-related issues. Parents, on the other hand, not only believe it is superficial and unnecessary to verbalize thoughts and feelings but they often do not have the skills to communicate effectively with their children.

Decision Making

One of the greatest sources of parent/child conflict among Korean Americans is the children's lack of control and decision-making power in their lives. As described earlier, Korean American students are often driven by parental shame and guilt due to their strong sense of obligation to obey their parents. Children are often reminded that parental struggle and sacrifice are to provide a better life for the children than they had. There is a strong sense of obligation to please parents and meet their expectations out of guilt, often stemming from the belief that parents have suffered and sacrificed their happiness for their children.

This is particularly reflected in young people's choice of college and career. Many Korean American students feel forced to major in academic areas that are of no interest to them. Typically, parents decide that their children will hold respectable positions such as lawyers, doctors, engineers, and accountants. Therefore, they are encouraged to pursue majors in medicine, science, law, and math-related fields. A study of Korean American college students in Los Angeles, for example, indicates that Korean American male students tend to major in the fields of physical science, engineering, and business (Song, 1982). The study also suggested that their degree of English proficiency was a significant factor in choosing majors that required less verbal skills. As a rule, standardized test scores for Korean Americans indicate significantly higher quantitative ability than verbal ability.

Counselors, however, need to keep in mind that in addition to language difficulties, many students pursue these fields because they are pressured by their parents. Many Korean American young people feel they have no control over their future and what they personally want to accomplish. For some, there is no room for negotiation, compromise, or change. They believe it is their responsibility to please and take care of their parents. Although it may be a logical move to encourage them to pursue their personal interests, many Korean American students feel trapped by their strongly internalized and deep-rooted cultural obligation.

Counseling Korean American Students

In counseling Korean American students, it is important first to assess their degree of adjustment and acculturation. There are varying levels of cultural identification and acculturation among Korean American students, depending on their age at immigration, parental values, and geographic location of residence (Lee & Cynn, 1991). According to Lee and Cynn (1991), integrating contradictory notions in Korean and American value systems into a unified identity is a primary challenge for Korean American students. Therefore, it is critical to understand their level of cultural identification to develop acculturation-consistent treatment strategies.

Effective intervention with Korean American students is unlikely without the involvement of the parents. Regardless of their level of acculturation, parents play a major role in influencing a child's self-concept and identity. As discussed throughout the chapter, it is the conflict between the child and the parent that is a major contributor to low self-esteem, emotional problems, and destructive behaviors. Parents can play a critical role in the counseling process as long as they are willing to make some changes in their parenting style and openly share their own difficulties, concerns, and love for their children.

Getting parent participation in counseling is perhaps the greatest challenge faced by counselors working with Korean American students. Due to family shame and stigma typically attached to mental health assistance, parents and students alike will often reject or deny the need for counseling until the problem has become severe and out of control. In addition, many parents view counseling as a reflection of their failure as parents. Not surprisingly, Korean American students seldom seek counseling services voluntarily. In many instances, they are forced to receive mental health assistance as a result of their involvement in illegal activities and/or as a condition of probation.

It is important that counselors be sensitive to parental resistance to counseling while promoting parent participation. One way of doing this is to explain the role of counseling and the function of the counselor. It should be done in such a way as to normalize the situation as an adjustment process and to dispel traditional myths about psychological assistance. Students also need to be reassured that adjustment-related difficulties are a normal process that many immigrants experience. Counselors also need to spend a considerable amount of time emphasizing client confidentiality. Students and parents alike need to be assured that they will not "lose face" or be "found out" by others in the community. Parents are often afraid that counseling will negatively affect their children's academic and career opportunities due to the record-keeping process. It is important for parents to be reassured that counseling is confidential and will not affect a child's life in society.

In cases where parental involvement is not possible, the role of school counselors becomes more challenging. Counselors need to understand that if they cannot work with the parents, it is difficult to change the student's family situation. Many Korean American students cannot view themselves separately and make decisions without family involvement. It is important for counselors to help students understand that although they may not change the views and values of their parents, they need to find outlets to vent their frustration and anger constructively. Also, helping them to understand the source of their cultural conflict and providing stress management and conflict resolution skills will promote their overall identity development.

Korean American parents may need to be encouraged to participate in parent education classes or support groups. Often, those parents who are resistant to receiving individual counseling may be more responsive to such education-related services. If limited English ability is an issue, it may be critical for counselors to identify community organizations or mental health service providers who are able to offer supportive services for the parents in their native language. Such classes and support groups need to be highly structured while providing a safe environment for parents to openly disclose their frustrations and concerns. Some of the topics to be covered might include communication skills, American youth culture, conflict resolution, stress and anger management, the U.S. educational system, alternative methods to corporal punishment, and child abuse laws and regulations in the United States.

Support groups for Korean American students can be a culturally responsive technique for dealing with the issues of acculturation and parent conflict. A group environment can reduce feelings of alienation and may assure students that they are not alone in their struggle to adjust to the new culture. It can also serve to alleviate their anxieties about counseling as they interact with other Korean students dealing with similar issues. It is critical for students to be in an environment where they can express their frustrations and anger that have often accumulated at home. Counselors need to provide Korean American students with constructive ways to manage anger and stress, along with skills in communication, conflict resolution, prejudice reduction, and increased awareness of ethnic relations and the acculturation process.

CASE STUDY

Young

Young is a 16-year-old Korean American male who immigrated to the United States three years ago with his parents and two younger sisters. His parents felt educational opportunity was limited in Korea, so they decided to move to the United States to provide a better future for their children. Upon arrival, the family moved into an apartment located in Koreatown in Los Angeles. Young's father and mother both work full time as liquor store owners until late in the evening and hardly have time to spend with their children. Young and his two sisters, ages 11 and 13, have spent their years in the United States mostly by themselves, unsupervised due to their parents' work schedules. As the oldest son, Young has been put in charge of taking care of his sisters and managing the house in his parents' absence.

In Korea, Young was always one of the best students in his class and very popular among his peers. As a sophomore in the United States, however, he has been struggling to keep up with his studies. His parents have made it very clear that he must achieve straight As. Last year, he completed his final English as a Second Language (ESL) course and is having difficulty maintaining an overall C average. He has a hard time understanding the teacher and has been daydreaming in his classes. As he slowly loses interest in school, he starts skipping classes. He later meets friends who encourage him to skip school and engage in illegal activities, including car theft.

His parents are unaware of his low grades, truancy, and illegal activities. Young managed to illegally change his grades in order to please his parents and conceal his true academic performance. He also faked his parents' signatures that were required for his absences. Young's parents found out about his failing grades and absences through a telephone call from one of his teachers. His father was so shocked and angered by this news that he forbade Young to leave the house after school or get involved in any activities outside of schoolwork. His sisters were to inform the father if Young did not come home. Out of concern that Young will continue to perform poorly, the father started lecturing Young daily about the importance of school, and reminding him of their hard work and sacrifice in coming to this country. His father also frequently compared Young with his sisters and family acquaintances who excel in school.

Initially, Young sat silently and listened to his father. As the lectures continued, Young became angry and started screaming at his father to leave him alone. Young ran out of the house out of fear that his father would strike him and did not come home for a few days. Currently, the father refuses to talk to Young and has stated that he is no longer his son. Meanwhile, Young is failing all his classes and has fallen deeper into his illegal involvement with his friends. He is easily angered and agitated, and contemplates dropping out of school since he sees no future for himself. He sees a school counselor to ask about his options and possible job-training opportunities.

This case illustrates a recent immigrant Korean American student experiencing serious adjustment difficulties primarily due to cultural conflict with his parents. It is critical to build rapport and gain a sense of trust from such a student before recommending counseling. Due to the stigma attached to mental health assistance, Young may be easily turned off and not return to the counselor's office. Therefore, a counselor needs to spend a considerable amount of time explaining the role and function of counseling and how it may benefit him. It will also be helpful for Young to understand that many immigrant students experience similar difficulties in school and with their parents in the adjustment and acculturation process.

Parental involvement is critical for effective intervention. It will be a challenge for the counselor to convince Young that it is important to involve his parents in the counseling process. Many Korean American students are appalled by the idea of involving their parents for fear of shaming the family and increasing the parental conflict. Young must be convinced that unless he and his parents try to understand and communicate with one another, the family situation will not improve.

Due to Young's parents' long working hours, it may only be possible to have several consultations with them rather than counseling. When calling the parents, it is important to urge the father to attend, since he is the decision maker and the main person in conflict with Young. Typically, the Korean American father will send the mother as the family representative, not only because of his limited English facility but also out of his shame and embarrassment. In an effort to reduce his anxiety, it may be appropriate not to mention the term *counseling* or *mental health* when arranging a meeting. Young's father will be more willing to participate if it is explained that such a meeting is needed to improve Young's academic performance. Because of the parents' strong emphasis on education, they will probably be more motivated to come in for a consultation on that topic.

The father needs to understand that Young cannot become an A student overnight. Progress is not only gradual but emotional support and encouragement is needed to help Young achieve his goals. The difficulty in learning a new language, adjusting to a new culture, and forming a bicultural identity must be shared. It would be important to emphasize that excellence in school performance is difficult without the parents' emotional support and encouragement during Young's process of adjustment.

Young's main reason for running away was the fear of being beaten—an acceptable method of punishment in Korea. His parents must learn that corporal punishment is against the law in the United States. Many Korean parents who immigrate to this country often do not understand the consequences of corporal punishment. The counselor, however, needs to respect traditional disciplinary practices. He or she should explain that, although it may be a respectable method of child rearing in Korea, it is prohibited in the United States and can result in grave consequences. Since this is the only method of discipline for a majority of parents in Korea, it is critical for counselors to explain alternative disciplinary methods.

Teaching his parents how to communicate with Young is a priority. The father, especially, needs to understand that although it may be considered disrespectful of Young to openly express his thoughts and feelings, there is a greater consequence if he remains silent. The father should be carefully reminded that Young is no longer a typical Korean son. He is now a Korean *American* son. While emphasizing the need for Young to have a high ethnic identification, it must be pointed out that it is also important for him to identify with the mainstream culture if he is to be a fully functioning bicultural individual. Encouraging Young to share his thoughts and feelings with his parents about his schoolwork and outside activities is important. In addition, the damaging effect of making comparisons and negative statements about Young must also be pointed out to the parents.

Such suggestions to parents need to be done in a way that does not undermine the appropriateness of their efforts. For example, Young's parents could be told that Young is very fortunate to have parents who care so deeply about his future and his well-being. The counselor could then explain to them that because they are dealing with a son who is in the process of learning to adjust to a new culture, they may need to be creative and try different methods to achieve positive results. Again, the situation can be normalized by telling them that immigrant parents are often faced with such challenges and often struggle with their children because of a conflict in cultures. Typically, parents view counselors as school authority figures who have all the answers and will be able to "fix" their children. Therefore, it is essential to empower the parents by emphasizing the importance of their role in working with Young. Moreover, it must be stressed that without their support and input, the counselor's efforts will not be effective.

In working with Young individually, the counselor first needs to provide an environment where Young can process his anger and frustration. It will be critical for Young to verbalize his thoughts and feelings and learn ways to deal with them constructively. Effective communication skills and anger management training might be appropriate to prevent Young from shouting at his father in times of conflict. As painful as it may be, it will be helpful for Young to realize that learning to understand and resolve these conflicts is an important part of the acculturation process. Both negative and positive aspects of Korean and American culture need to be fully explored to clarify the forces influencing identity development in order to provide a student such as Young the opportunity to define his own identity (Lee & Cynn, 1991).

There is a great sense of loss that immigrant students feel in leaving behind their friends and relatives in their native country. Many do not have the opportunity to process their loss and feelings of grief. They are often told to forget about the past and to concentrate on their future and do well in school. Young was one of the top students in his class in Korea. Since he was doing very well and had many close friends, it is possible that he did not share his parents' desire to immigrate to the United States. Therefore, it will be important to process his lifestyle, friends, and school life in Korea, and the family's reasons for immigrating for the counselor to fully understand Young's position and to help him set new meaningful life goals.

Young's involvement in illegal activities needs to be addressed next. The legal consequences and potential damage to his future opportunities as a result of these activities must be pointed out. It will help Young to understand that his involvement is largely out of anger toward his family and his desire to be accepted by his peers. Young may benefit from assertiveness training as a result of his vulnerability to peer pressure. Finding a student mentor who has had similar experiences or enrolling him in a peer support group may be extremely helpful in providing support and reducing Young's feelings of alienation and hopelessness. Korean American students will generally respond to a structured group that is based on skillbuilding. Open-ended, feeling-oriented, processing groups are often too ambiguous and threatening for students who are initially resistant to disclosing feelings, particularly those related to family problems.

It will be important for Young to understand that increase in school performance is a gradual process that may take extra time and effort. Young will need assistance in setting obtainable academic goals to gradually improve his grades. He lost interest in school because he could not meet parental expectations and saw no hope for his future. The counselor may want to reinforce even the slightest improvement in academic performance and urge the parents to do the same. Often, even after improvement, many Korean American students are not impressed or proud of themselves because they may still fall short of parental expectations. The counselor needs to challenge his all-or-nothing thinking about not having a promising future because of his poor grades in school. It is important for the counselor to help Young understand that his thinking comes largely from his parents and is not an accurate reflection of his true potential and future opportunities.

Conclusion

Korean American students experience a wide range of adjustment-related problems mainly due to the cultural conflict with their parents. In addition to the developmental challenges of the adolescent years, they are forced to develop an identity within two opposing cultures and value systems. The counselor's knowledge and understanding of the source of cultural conflict will be critical for effective intervention with the family. Furthermore, empowering parents through their input and participation in the counseling process will be essential to the overall outcome. Korean American students and parents need significant support and encouragement in their efforts to adjust and understand the new culture and the educational system. It is important for counselors to help Korean American students develop cultural awareness and skills—for example, communication, conflict resolution, and stress and anger management— that can serve to facilitate the adjustment process.

A SPECIAL CHALLENGE: RECENT IMMIGRANT AND REFUGEE YOUTH FROM SOUTHEAST ASIA

Youth who are recent immigrants or refugees from countries in Southeast Asia may present some special challenges to school counselors. Many immigrants from Southeast Asia must deal with the trauma of the refugee experience and the stress of resettlement and adjustment in the United States (Chung & Okazaki, 1991). Young people who are refugees from Southeast Asia have often experienced deprivation, physical injury, torture, and incarceration on their journey to the United States (Mollica, Wyshak, Coelho, & Lavelle, 1985). After an arduous journey, many of these young people and their families must then deal with the stress of meeting their basic needs and adapting to a new country and culture (Tayabas & Pok, 1983).

Young people who immigrate from Southeast Asia may therefore be in need of significant counseling intervention. However, they may not come for counseling for a combination of reasons. Fear, often generated by the trauma and stress of their refugee experience, may make students reluctant to become involved with a counselor—a perceived agent of the social order. In addition, there may be a lack of understanding about counseling services among students and their parents. In many instances, the concept of *mental health* is foreign to Southeast Asian immigrants because traditional Southeast Asian culture does not distinguish between the treatment of physical problems and psychological concerns (Chung & Okazaki, 1991; Lin & Masuda,

1983). Counselors need to be mindful of the fact that they may face a major task in attempting to establish trust and credibility with this student population.

Counseling students who have immigrated from Southeast Asia may require the coordination of a number of social service resources. The school counselor, therefore, may need to seek the assistance of other social and community agencies to help students and their families address issues such as housing, employment, and welfare. It might also be important to provide guidance in helping students and their parents gain English language proficiency. Significantly, success in coordinating such services may serve to promote trust in and credibility for school counseling services among students and their parents.

Hinsvark (1989–90) described a model intervention program in an urban school district that uses Southeast Asian guidance aides. These aides are paraprofessionals from the community who provide assistance to the school counselors in promoting the academic, career, and psychosocial development of Southeast Asian students. These bilingual/bicultural aides serve as role models for recently arrived Southeast Asian students. They serve as interpreters, translating not only the new language but the new culture as well. They also mediate cultural conflicts that may arise between students, parents, and the counselors. In consultation with the school counselor, they develop a four-year academic and career plan with Southeast Asian eighth-grade students and their parents, and a two-year academic and career plan with all Southeast Asian tenth-grade students and their parents.

Counseling students of Southeast Asian descent can be a major task for the school counseling professional. Working with this student population requires cultural sensitivity as well as the ability to coordinate a variety of helping resources.

CONCLUSION

School counseling professionals must be prepared to address the developmental needs of the rapidly increasing number of students of Asian descent. They must get beyond the myth of the model minority and the stereotypes associated with it. In order to do this, they must become familiar with the varied cultural and historical dynamics that shape the personality of Asian American students. This chapter has attempted to outline some background information, guidelines, and suggestions essential for counseling Asian American young people in the nation's schools.

REFERENCES

Asian and Pacific Islander Advisory Committee. (1988). *Final report.* Sacramento, CA: Attorney General.

Atkinson, D., Morten, G., & Sue, D. W. (in press). *Counseling American minorities: A cross-cultural perspective.* Dubuque, IA: Brown.

Bempechat, J., & Omori, M. C. (1988). *Meeting the educational needs of Southeast Asian children.* New York: Columbia University, Teachers College. (Eric Document Reproduction Service No. ED 328 644).

Chung, R. C., & Okazaki, S. (1991). Counseling Americans of Southeast Asian descent. In C. C. Lee & B. L. Richardson (Eds.), *Multicultural issues in counseling: New approaches to diversity* (pp. 107–126). Alexandria, VA: American Association for Counseling and Development.

Ford, R. (1983). *Counseling strategies for ethnic minority students* (pp. 1–43). University of Puget Sound.

Hartman, J. S., & Askounis, A. C. (1989). Asian American students: Are they really a "model minority"? *The School Counselor, 37,* 109–112.

Hinsvark, D. (1989–90). Cross-cultural counseling by Southeast Asian guidance aides. *California Association of Counseling and Development Journal, 10,* 21–28.

Izawa, C. (1988). *Educational excellence of Asian Americans: Myth or reality? A perspective of an Asian/American Academician.* In S. Karkhanis & B. Tsai (Eds.), Papers presented at the American Library Association Convention (pp. 18–23).

Karkhanis, S., & Tsai, B. (Eds.). (1988). Papers presented at the American Library Association Convention (pp. 18–23).

Lee, J. C., & Cynn, V. E. H. (1991). Issues in counseling 1.5 generation Korean Americans. In C. C. Lee & B. L. Richardson (Eds.), *Multicultural issues in counseling: New approaches to diversity* (pp. 127–140). Alexandria, VA: American Association for Counseling and Development.

Lin, K. M., & Masuda, M. (1983). Impact of the refugee experience: Mental health issues of the Southeast Asians. In *Bridging cultures: Southeast Asian refugees in America* (pp. 32–52). Los Angeles: Special Services for Groups—Asian American Community Mental Health Training Center.

Mollica, R. F., Wyshak, G., Coelho, R., & Lavelle, J. (1985). *The Southeast Asian psychiatry patient: A treatment outcome study.* Boston: Indochinese Psychiatric Clinic.

Morrow, R. D. (1989). Southeast-Asian parental involvement: Can it be a reality? *Elementary School Guidance and Counseling, 23,* 289–297.

Olson, L. (1988). *Crossing the schoolhouse border: Immigrant students and the California public schools.* San Francisco, CA: California Tomorrow.

Rong, X., & Preissle-Goetz, J. (1990). *High school dropouts among foreign born whites, Hispanics, and Asians.* Paper presented at the meeting of the American Educational Research Association, Boston, MA.

Shon, S. P., & Ja, D. Y. (1982). Asian families. In M. McGoldrick, J. K. Pearce, & J. Giordano (Eds.), *Ethnicity and family therapy* (pp. 208–228). New York: Guilford Press.

Song, D. S. (1982). Korean College Students in Los Angeles: Basic Characteristics. In Yu, Philips, & Yang (Eds.), *Koreans in Los Angeles: Prospects and promises* (pp. 133–153). Los Angeles: Center for Korean-American and Korean Studies, California State University, Los Angeles.

Sue, D. W. (1981). *Counseling the culturally different: Theory and practice.* New York: Wiley.

Sue, D. W., & Sue, D. *(1990). Counseling the culturally different: Theory and practice* (2nd ed.). New York: Wiley.

Sue, S., & Sue, D. W. (1991). Counseling strategies for Chinese Americans. In C. C. Lee & B. L. Richardson (Eds.), *Multicultural issues in counseling: New approaches to diversity* (pp. 79–80). Alexandria, VA: American Association for Counseling and Development.

Suzuki, B. (1990). Asian Americans on campus: Breaking the silence. In R. Gross (Con. Ed.), *Focus, 4* (2), 1–3.

Tayabas, T., & Pok, T. (1983). The arrival of the Southeast Asian refugees in America: An overview. In *Bridging cultures: Southeast Asian refugees in America* (pp. 3–14). Los Angeles: Special Services for Groups—Asian American Community Mental Health Training Center.

Yao, E. L. (1985). Adjustment needs of Asian immigrant children. *Elementary School Guidance and Counseling, 19* (3), 222–227.

Yu, E. Y. (1987). Causes of juvenile delinquency. *Juvenile delinquency in the Korean community of Los Angeles* (pp. 40–62). Los Angeles: Korea Times.

Yu, E. Y. (1990). *Korean community profile* (pp. 1–6). Los Angeles: Korea Times.

ADDITIONAL RESOURCES FOR COUNSELING ASIAN AMERICAN STUDENTS

Austin, G. A., Prendergast, M. L., & Lee, H. (1989). *Substance abuse among Asian American youth* (Prevention Research Update No. 5). Portland, OR: Northwest Regional Educational Laboratory.

Ching, W., & Presen, S. (1980). Asian Americans in group counseling: A case of cultural dissonance. *Journal for Specialists in Group Work, 5*, 228–232.

Coon, D. L., & Emonds, R. M. (Eds.). (1982). *Indochinese refugees.* Provo, UT: Brigham Young University

Dinh Te, H. (1988). *The Indochinese and their cultures.* San Diego: The Multifunctional Resource Center, Policy Studies Department, College of Education, San Diego State University.

Reynolds, D. K. (1980). *Quiet therapies.* Honolulu: The University Press of Hawaii.

Sue, D. (1980). Asian-American. In N. A. Vacc & J. P. Wittmer (Eds.), *Let me be me* (pp. 175–195). Muncie, IN: Accelerated Development.

Yip, B. C. (1985). A culturally sensitive approach to primary prevention: The Pan Asian model. *Family Resource Coalition Report, 5*, 8–9.

5

COUNSELING HISPANIC CHILDREN AND YOUTH

JESSE T. ZAPATA

INTRODUCTION

Research and writing about counseling and minorities continue to be of importance to the counseling profession. Recently, the *Journal of Counseling and Development* devoted an entire issue to "Multiculturalism as a Fourth Force in Counseling." For Hispanics, it is critical that the counseling profession continue its efforts to deal with those issues. Hispanics are developing an increasing presence in the United States. This presence is numerical, psychological, and cultural. By the year 2000, the Hispanic proportion of the U.S. population is expected to increase to between 8.6 and 9.9 percent (Orum, 1986). Large Hispanic communities exist in practically every major city in the country. School populations are becoming increasingly Hispanic; however, the school teaching and counseling population remains primarily white. Cross-cultural counseling issues continue to need addressing, both in the preservice and in-service training of school counselors. Unfortunately, there is no clear agreement among counselor educators regarding what to teach, or even how to teach about Hispanics.

The confusion is partly related to the fact that heterogeneity within ethnic groups is often ignored in the research that counselors study in their training programs. In addition, similarities and differences between Hispanic subgroups often are ignored. The latter issue concerns the fact that people referred to as Hispanic can have very different historical and cultural characteristics. Hispanic communities exist in every major city in the country, but different subgroups predominate in different localities. Although similar in many ways, Hispanics are also very heterogeneous in terms of social and educational background, history, and culture. Generally included in this group are people from Mexico, Central and South America, and those from the three major Caribbean islands (Cuba, Puerto Rico, and the Dominican Republic), with a culture from Spain and immigrants directly from the Iberian peninsula to the United States.

Highlights about Hispanics, from *The Hispanic Population in the United States: March 1989* (del Pinal & DeNavas, 1990), indicate that the Hispanic population, which totaled 20.1 million in March of 1989, continues to grow rapidly—about five times faster than the rate of the non-Hispanic population since 1980. Immigration was an important factor in that growth, contributing to about one-half of the expansion. In addition, Hispanics were more likely than non-Hispanics to live in urban areas and more likely to be poor. Some 24 percent of Hispanic families fall below the poverty level, compared with 9 percent of non-Hispanic families. Moreover, 65 percent of the Hispanic population is concentrated in three states (California, Texas, and New York), with additional Hispanics residing in Florida (8 percent), Illinois and Arizona (4 percent), New Jersey and New Mexico (3 percent), and Colorado (2 percent).

Mexican Americans are the largest and most prominent group of Hispanics. Mexican-origin Hispanics (about 12.5 million) account for about 63 percent of the Hispanic population in the United States. Approximately 80 percent of them live in the Southwest, mostly in urban areas. Both the history and culture of Mexican Americans have long been closely tied to the Southwest. This long history, together with an "invisible border," foster continual movement between Mexico and the United States. This sustained immigration has reduced the need for Mexican Americans to "acculturate" in the same manner as other immigrants have done.

Large-scale migration of Puerto Ricans did not begin until after World War II. The number of Puerto Ricans living on the mainland increased from 300,000 in 1950 to 1.4 million in 1970, and 2.6 million in 1985 (Orum, 1986). Puerto Ricans are the hardest hit of any Hispanic group. They consistently are the least educated, more often unemployed, and more likely to be poor (Barreto, 1986). This is partly explained by the population's circular migration that limits the establishment of a firm foothold in either the mainland's or the island's economy (Carrasquillo, 1991).

There are about one million Cubans in the United States. Most live in southern Florida, but large numbers reside in New York City, Chicago, Los Angeles, Boston, and New Jersey (Orum, 1986). Of the three largest Hispanic subgroups in the United States, Cubans probably possess the greatest economic power (Arredondo, 1991). However, they still experience many of the problems associated with other Hispanic groups, such as immigration, acculturation, and social deprivation (Gonzalez, 1991).

Increasing numbers of immigrants from Central and South America are entering the United States. In 1950, the number of Central and South Americans in the country was estimated at 57,000. In 1985, 1.7 million Central and South Americans were identified, as well as 1.4 million "other Hispanics" (Orum, 1986).

PSYCHOSOCIAL DEVELOPMENT OF HISPANIC YOUTH

Several variables influence the way in which Hispanic children develop. Cultural and socioeconomic variables affect this development, but their respective impacts are often difficult to confirm. Early writers on Hispanics emphasized simplistic views of Hispanic children and their families. These views invariably arose from ethnocentric researchers who began with narrow assumptions about how Hispanics differed from Whites. In time, further refined research approaches resulted in a more sophisticated perspective regarding Hispanic students.

Early researchers tended to emphasize cultural differences between Hispanics and whites. Concurrently, they tended to deemphasize or ignore other significant variables (such as educational, occupational, and economic levels of their subjects). This approach resulted in long lists of cultural characteristics that were then presumed to differentiate Hispanics from whites. When research findings did not support the presumed differences, researchers concluded that the results reflected the influence of the acculturation process and thus ignored the possibility that the presumed differences may not have existed in the first place.

Current researchers and writers are more likely to account for variables that may influence the results of their investigations. They at least acknowledge and often control for socioeconomic variables that affect the psychological and social development of Hispanic children and youth and are less likely to attribute that development to cultural characteristics that have not been empirically supported. Nevertheless, several traits are often ascribed to Hispanic families that, in fact, describe families with low socioeconomic status.

It can be argued that economic problems are critical issues for Hispanics. The problems are especially critical for large families headed by females, as these families tend to be poor. For the most part, they are a very young population, with a high birth rate and a low level of educational attainment. They tend to work in low-skill jobs, receive low wages, and experience high rates of under- and unemployment. These economic problems often subsequently result in social milieu stressors for Hispanic youth who experience the impact of poverty, unemployment, and underemployment, as well as discrimination (Schinke, Moncher, Palleja, Zayas, & Schilling, 1988).

Socioeconomic characteristics of Hispanic families do indeed influence the development of Hispanic children, but Hispanic cultural and historical characteristics also have an impact on that development. As indicated earlier, however, it is difficult to isolate cultural variables from socioeconomic ones. Confusing and contradictory findings still persist in the literature. In many cases, constructs that were approached in a simplistic fashion are, in fact, more complex than previously assumed.

Three variables commonly attributed to Hispanics, which empirical research has demonstrated either as erroneous or far more complex than early researchers believed, are briefly reviewed as examples of problems with respect to research on Hispanics. These variables include fatalism and two characteristics commonly used to described Hispanic families: "machismo" and familism.

Fatalism, and related forms of passivity, are often attributed to Hispanics (especially Mexican Americans), yet the research on locus of control (a psychological construct with being "externally controlled," presumably related to fatalism) yielded inconsistent results when applied to Hispanics as early as the 1960s. By the 1970s, several authors had demonstrated that Hispanics were more "internal" than whites. Garza and Ames (1974), for example, demonstrated that Mexican American college students were less "external" than whites on the luck/fate dimensions of locus of control. The locus of control research on school-age children has reported a trend toward greater "internality" among white children, but the results are often inconsistent and even contradictory, perhaps reflecting researchers' tendency to fail to control for socioeconomic variables (Shorr & Young, 1984).

Machismo, or the male dominance often ascribed to Hispanic families (Mexican American families in particular), is a good example of how observations made by early researchers have often become embedded both in psychological and popular belief systems. A long line of studies on male dominance in the Hispanic culture leads to the following conclusions: (1) the male dominance reported by the early researchers has been greatly exaggerated; (2) no difference exists in power structures of Mexican American and white families; (3) joint decision making typifies Mexican American families; (4) no difference exists between Mexican American and white families with respect to task differentiation (Hartzler & Franco, 1985).

A final trait commonly attributed to Hispanics is *familism.* Sabogal, Marin, Otero-Sabogal, VanOss, and Perez-Stable (1987) stated that familism has been defined as the degree to which individuals feel a strong identification and attachment with their families (nuclear and extended). These authors did conclude that familism is an important core characteristic for Hispanics (Mexican, Central, and Cuban Americans). Familism is composed of multiple dimensions, however—some of which seem to persist across generations, and some of which differentiate between "acculturated" Hispanics and whites.

STATUS OF HISPANIC YOUTH IN THE SCHOOLS

Counselors must have a clear understanding of the characteristics of Hispanic children and youth if school counseling programs are to meet their needs effectively. The youthfulness of the Hispanic population makes this understanding critical. In 1989, 35 percent of the Hispanic population was under 18 years of age, compared with 25 percent of the population not of Hispanic origin (del Pinal & DeNavas 1990). Between 1960 and 1985, there was a decline in the proportion of white students and a rise in the proportion of minority students. The proportion of Hispanic students increased at each level of education from 1975 to 1985. Hispanics showed proportionately larger increases than blacks in elementary and high school enrollment (U.S. Department of Education, 1988).

A brief review of the research on Hispanic students, in terms of their school performance, makes it clear that there are many areas in which school counselors can have a tremendous impact. For example, the educational achievement of Hispanics, with the exception of Cubans, is generally lower than that of the (general) non-Hispanic population (Zavaleta, 1981). The school dropout rates for Hispanics is about 28 percent, for blacks about 15 percent, and for whites about 12 percent (U.S. Department of Education, 1988). Additional areas in which school counselors can have an impact concern personal and social variables related to Hispanic children and youth. These variables include the development of cultural identity and self-concept within an often hostile environment and the attainment of status within the school's social structure.

The processes of acculturation and assimilation, as well as the development of ethnic and cultural identity, have recently begun to receive more attention in the psychological and counseling literature. The concepts of acculturation and ethnic identity have evolved into rather complex constructs regarding how Hispanics interact with the dominant culture and develop personal identity. Early concepts of acculturation described the process as a linear one and ignored the many factors that impact the individual in adjusting to a complex world. Today, acculturation is best conceptualized as a multidimensional and multidirectional process whereby ethnic minorities learn to live and survive in the modern world (Garza & Gallegos, 1985). Ethnic identity development usually refers to issues of self-image and perceptions of one's own ethnic group as related to attitudes, beliefs, and feelings for the dominant culture. Such development can impact Hispanic children's interactions with peers and teachers, as well as their long-term life and career development (Baron, 1991).

Hispanic children and youth are often presumed by teachers and counselors to have poor self-concepts. The research on self-concept with respect to Hispanic students, however, has produced mixed results. Martinez and Dukes (1987) reported that research in the 1940s and 1950s found that dominant group members had better self-concepts than minorities. Many studies in the 1960s and 1970s reported that race was not related to self-concept; and yet other studies from the 1970s and 1980s did find differences related to race or ethnicity. These last studies, however, demonstrated that self-concept consists of a multitude of evaluations on different traits. In their study, for example, Martinez and Dukes found that Hispanic middle and high school students tended to have lower levels of self-esteem than whites on public domain traits, but that this pattern does not hold for private domain traits. More specifically, these students tended to have lower self-concepts than whites when the domain under examination was school-related (achievement, ability, intelligence), but higher self-concepts than whites when the domain under examination was more personally oriented.

That Hispanic students often perceive and probably experience school differently from white students is further supported by research related to school environments and policies. The ethnic mix of students, for example, seems to impact on a school's climate as perceived by teachers (Pallas, 1988). Specifically, teachers in schools with higher percentages of minority students tend to perceive greater administrative control, less teacher control over the classroom and school policies, and worse student behavior. A mediating variable in the development of these perceptions might be the extent to which schools emphasize multicultural curricula, the recruitment of a multicultural staff, and the involvement of minority parents. Schools high on this variable ("high equity" schools) have a positive impact on the degree to which teachers and students attribute leadership characteristics to Hispanic students (Moore, 1988). Lastly, Strodl (1988) found that students from different ethnic backgrounds responded differently to a mutually experienced environment. This suggests that it is important for school counselors to be attuned to the possible differences within their schools.

Hispanic students may also be impacted differently by the school's disciplinary procedures. According to data reported by the Office of Civil Rights of the Department of Education (1987), the degree to which corporal punishment is used with minority students increases as the percentage of minority students in the school increases. In addition, a study conducted by this author (Zapata, 1990) in a metropolitan Texas school district demonstrated that the use of corporal punishment tended to increase as the Hispanic student population grew at the elementary and middle school levels.

Although it is evident that Hispanic and white students can experience the same school environment differently and that there are actual differences in how students are treated within those schools, it is wrong to conclude that all Hispanic groups view and experience school in exactly the same way. There are within-group differences. As an example, school dropout rates for Mexican American and Puerto Rican children have reached alarming proportions in many areas of the country, yet Cuban children experience this problem less frequently (Zavaleta, 1981). In addition, variables commonly associated with dropping out (cutting classes, suspensions, dating, being older, being female, disciplinary problems) are represented in various Hispanic groups in different ways (Velez, 1989).

Fernandez (1989) attempted to determine differences and similarities among major Hispanic high school ninth-graders enrolled in predominately minority high schools in major U.S. cities. He indentified 24 similarities and 17 differences among four Hispanic groups (Mexican American, Puerto Rican, Cuban, Central American), reinforcing the notion that generalizations across Hispanic groups can be misleading. Similarities across the Hispanic groups suggest that Hispanic students choose Hispanic friends; like school; recognize that good study habits are important for school success but admit friends and peers may be impediments to success in school; discuss school and personal problems with friends and parents *more than* with school teachers or counselors; receive most of their advice to stay in school from their mothers or stepmothers and their teachers; believe that a good job and future life success depend on finishing high school; and have parents who probably did not finish high school but expect their children to graduate. Additionally, although parents tended to speak only Spanish at home, they strongly encouraged their children to learn both English and Spanish.

Differences among the Hispanic groups include the degree to which English is used at school and with friends; classmates are perceived as valuing school; classmates are perceived as valuing regular attendance and following school rules; and teachers are perceived as expecting good behavior.

A final area that school counselors need to understand more fully relative to Hispanic students is career development. Despite background limitations, Hispanic students' aspirations tend to be about the same as those of Anglo students (Chahin, 1983; Hispanic Research Center, 1991); however, their school experiences tend to limit their opportunities (Ascher, 1985). According to Ascher, 40 percent of all Hispanic high school students are in a general track, 35 percent are in vocational programs, and only 25 percent are in an academic track.

Hispanic children and youth have a difficult experience in public school, which exacerbates obstacles in life and career development. Sociologically and economically oriented career perspectives are probably more helpful than personality based ones in understanding that development. This point is illustrated by data indicating that Hispanic men are more likely to be employed in operator, fabricator, and laborer occupations than in any other occupation group, whereas non-Hispanic men tend to be employed in managerial and professional occupations (del Pinal & DeNavas 1990). Similarly, Hispanic women tend to be employed in service occupations more often than non-Hispanic women who tend to be employed in managerial and professional occupations. Income data from 1986 reveal a large gap, of at least 30 percent, between Hispanic incomes and those of white males (Barreto, 1986). Hispanic women who work full time have the lowest income of any population subgroup, earning $.51 to the dollar earned by white males. These data, coupled with other points presented, suggest that Hispanic children are subsequently severely limited in terms of economic support, occupational opportunity, and career role models. Additionally, the opportunity for Hispanics to break out of this cycle of poverty appears to be slim, since there is a severe mismatch between new jobs (white collar) being generated in the United States and those jobs (blue collar) in which most Hispanics are currently employed (Barreto, 1986).

DEVELOPING APPROPRIATE STRATEGIES FOR WORKING WITH HISPANIC CHILDREN AND YOUTH

Pederson (1988) suggested that one of the most frequently encountered examples of cultural bias or prejudice that appears in the literature on multicultural counseling is the assumption that counselors need to change individuals to fit the system versus changing the system to fit the individual. For Hispanic students, it is essential that school counselors challenge and strive to change this assumption. More recently, Cottone (1991) suggested that counselors should develop a systemic emphasis to their roles. That is, counselors should view client problems as being symbolic of larger contextual problems insofar as clients are intimately tied to their social relationships. Therefore, counselors must understand and analyze (1) the service delivery system, (2) the client's system(s) of influence, and (3) the counselor-client relationship as affected by both the service delivery and client systems. Therefore, counselors must be experts on the service delivery system that they represent. They must also be aware of their roles as transmitters of the culture from which that system springs.

A related problem is that too often school personnel simply forget or refuse to use sound planning procedures when dealing with minority issues. As an example, this author was asked to serve on a committee whose stated mission was to review the district's procedures for identifying, screening, and selecting participants for its gifted and talented programs. Of special concern was how minorities fared in this process. At the first two meetings of this committee, absolutely no data were presented from which strengths and weaknesses in the district's procedures could be identified relative to minorities. More distressing was the response the author received when he asked for the data; that is, that no data were necessary to accomplish the committee's charge. While it is hoped that the events described here are an extreme example, they do suggest that there often is hesitancy and resistance to bring potentially disturbing data to the surface.

And yet, careful examination of data and information about a school's clientele is a crucial first step in developing counseling programs responsive to the needs of Hispanic students. Minority children are likely to gain more from counseling programs when their counselors perceive their roles in a systemic fashion and when they are able to implement such an approach in their planning. Several authors have described procedures for developing comprehensive counseling programs. Gysbers and Henderson (1988) proposed a model for the development of a comprehensive school program, which is modified and streamlined here, as well as infused with a systemic perspective, to help counselors respond more appropriately to the needs of Hispanic students. The modified model includes four basic steps: assessing, designing, implementing, and evaluating. Counselors can take specific action in order to ensure that Hispanic students receive appropriate services by following the steps outlined by Gysbers and Henderson.

Assessing Needs of Hispanic Students

The first step in planning is to conduct a needs assessment with respect to Hispanic children and youth in a school population. General information about Hispanic children is a useful guide. In addition, information specific to a given school's population can be gathered within the framework of general concepts regarding Hispanic children and youth. It is important to remember, however, that there is heterogeneity both among and within various Hispanic groups. Thus, although counselors need to draw generalizations from the literature, such generalizations are mere guidelines for systematically assessing the characteristics and needs of the specific students with whom they are working. For example, these generalizations can help school counselors define the specific areas that should be assessed to develop programs that are more responsive to Hispanic students.

Since school counselors often do not have the time or the technical support to conduct formal needs assessments, this assessment can be informal. It can emphasize the major variables effecting the psychological development of Hispanic youth, including both socioeconomic and cultural ones. It can also focus on indicators of the status of Hispanic youth in the school, including school performance, acculturation and assimilation issues, self-esteem, school climate, disciplinary procedures, and career aspirations.

School counselors can identify the major socioeconomic variables effecting the physical and social development of Hispanic children and youth in the school. Formal and informal strategies for data collection can be utilized; for example; consider the following:

Formal Strategies

Obtain the percentage of Hispanic students on the school's free lunch program.

Determine the percentage of Hispanic students attending the school who live in public housing.

Obtain data on literacy, income, and housing from the city government, with respect to the neighborhoods served by the school.

Informal Strategies

Observe the number of Hispanic children obtaining free lunches.

Ask the school nurse to describe the frequency and types of health problems for which Hispanic students are referred.

The school counselor can develop a working hypothesis regarding Hispanic cultural values and family characteristics impacting the psychological development of Hispanic children and youth in the school by doing the following:

Formal Strategies

Review some of the research on Hispanic cultural values and family characteristics (references and resources are included in this chapter).

Ask a university professor (sociology, psychology, counseling) to conduct a study in the school's neighborhoods, focusing on Hispanic values and/or family characteristics.

Informal Strategies

Note whether both Hispanic parents attend counseling sessions or whether mothers or fathers attend alone. If both parents attend, who does the talking?

Note whether parents attending counseling sessions (or Individual Education Planning sessions, for example) have difficulty communicating in English. Would they prefer communicating in Spanish? Do they appear confused?

School counselors can also gather data regarding Hispanic children's academic, social, personal, and vocational development.

Formal Strategies

Collect data by ethnicity on leadership positions held and on selection for various school honors and/or participation in special school activities.

Review data by ethnicity on testing and selection for gifted programs, as well as on referrals for and selection for other special programs.

Review data on the use of corporal punishment and suspension.

Administer an acculturation scale to determine the degree to which Hispanic students have become acculturated and the degree to which they might be experiencing cultural stress.

Determine the degree to which Hispanics come for counseling and the kinds of problems that they bring.

Determine the degree to which Hispanic students are referred for counseling, by whom, and for what reasons.

Survey teachers and administrators regarding their perceptions of special problems faced by Hispanic students in the school.

Informal Strategies

Observe students in classes and note patterns of interaction. (Do they volunteer to answer questions? How do they interact with other students?)

Note your counseling style and its effectiveness with Hispanic students.

Ask students how they feel about the school, the teachers, and the administration.

Ask students how they believe Hispanics, blacks, and whites get along in the school.

The data gathered through these efforts should be reviewed with the following questions in mind:

- What do these data suggest about the school counseling program's responsiveness to the characteristics and needs of Hispanic students?
- What do these data suggest about the school staffs' perceptions of Hispanic students?
- What do these data suggest about how well the school counseling program is preparing Hispanic students for their future lives and careers?
- To what degree are problems experienced by Hispanic students a reflection of problems experienced by (1) students of the same age, (2) students in the same socioeconomic setting? To what degree might they be a reflection of society's treatment of Hispanic minorities?

Designing Programs Responsive to Hispanic Students

Analysis of the data gathered by school counselors can help guide them in designing interventions that match specific needs. Counselors should design programs for addressing needs uncovered during the needs assessment. In addition, school counselors should be willing to develop programs to help the school structure implement change, if the need for change is revealed in the needs assessment.

Programs can be aimed directly at helping students deal with their own issues, whether those issues are socioeconomic, educational, personal, or social. Programs can also target helping the school structure change to be more responsive to Hispanic students and their parents. School counselors developing programs for the former can:

- Identify students with leadership potential and conduct group sessions, focusing on the development of leadership skills and assertive behavior.
- Conduct classroom guidance sessions that help students understand cultural diversity and its dynamics, including the influence that groups have on each other and how culture changes over time.
- Conduct classroom guidance sessions that will help students understand similarities and differences between different ethnic and cultural groups, as well as within ethnic and cultural groups.
- Identify students who are at risk given the social milieu in which they live and offer individual and/or group counseling sessions aimed at helping them develop appropriate coping strategies for dealing with their difficulties. Cognitive-behavioral strategies are ideally suited for individuals experiencing problems associated with societal stressors.
- Ensure that career guidance programs broaden the experience base of students to facilitate better long-range planning. Personality-based theories are too narrow given the economic and sociological realities in which Hispanic students tend to live.

Counselors developing programs aimed at helping the school make appropriate changes can:

- Present teachers and the administration with the data collected during the assessment phase and engage them in discussions of those data and in developing appropriate institutional responses. The example presented earlier regarding the use of corporal punishment as related to the percent of Hispanic enrollments in the schools would provide an interesting catalyst for this type of discussion. Other possible problem areas include referral and selection for gifted and talented programs and referrals for disciplinary action.
- Conduct workshops with teachers aimed at helping them understand the socioeconomic and cultural characteristics of the students and their families.
- Offer parent consultation services during evening hours at locations that are convenient for the community. A school district in San Antonio, Texas, for example, offers these services to Hispanic parents in a shopping mall, as this was the most convenient location for parents from several different schools served by the program.

In a school where Hispanic students are not assuming leadership positions or tend to be underrepresented in visible and positive school programs and activities, the counselor could target those problems for resolution. The counselor's goal could be to increase the degree to which Hispanic students are involved in those positions or activities. The counselor would design a program for those students that would include the following steps:

1. *Identify Hispanic students with potential for involvement in leadership positions and/or school activities.* Teachers can be asked to list the names of students in their classes who could be effective leaders and/or be involved in school activities if given the opportunity. Students who offer hints of potential include those who:
    a. Volunteer ideas when not in front of their peers.
    b. Quietly volunteer for projects, perhaps after or before class.
    c. Surprise the teacher with their knowledge of current events.
    d. Do better on tests than the teacher expected.
    e. Do well on creative assignments or are creative problem solvers.

    f.   Are depended on by other students for support or guidance.

  2. *Recruit Hispanic students with leadership potential to participate in sessions designed to develop their leadership and participation skills.* The counselor could:

    a.   Invite the targeted students to a lunch meeting with the counselor.

    b.   Inform them about the theme for the sessions as well as specifics (how many weeks, during which classes, etc.).

  3. *Conduct a series of six sessions with a focus on helping the students view themselves as potential leaders and different ways in implementing that view:*

    a.   *Session 1:* Ask the participants to list the school's most involved students, with a focus on student leaders, and to discuss what characteristics these students possess. Help them talk about participation and leadership in general— what makes a person want to be involved and to be a leader in school activities?

    b.   *Session 2:* Encourage the students to talk about their perceptions of the involvement of Hispanic students in leadership positions in the school. Ask them to discuss whether they would like to be more involved in the school's activities. In preparation for the next session, ask the students to bring newspaper articles focusing on Hispanic leaders in the community.

    c.   *Session 3:* Invite two Hispanics noted for their leadership in the community to discuss early experiences that helped them develop their leadership and participation skills. Encourage students to ask questions and to discuss the articles they brought.

    d.   *Session 4:* Encourage the students to talk about how they can become more involved in the school's activities.

    e.   *Session 5:* Obtain a commitment from the students to implement their plan of action.

    f.   *Session 6:* Ask the students to report the results of their efforts to implement their plans. Help the students revise their plans, if necessary. Set dates for follow-up sessions.

Implementing Programs Responsive to Hispanic Students

Implementing the types of strategies outlined here requires that school counselors have a systemic view of the counseling role, as well as the ability to apply such a role. These counselors must be aware of their own cultural values and their own tendencies to view members of other ethnic or cultural groups in stereotypical ways. They must also be willing to confront their own limitations and to change.

In addition, many of the issues that will surface in the needs assessment phase of this process might cause discomfort in school, and therefore lead to some discomfort for the counselor. Some of the questions that would need addressing in the needs assessment might prove uncomfortable to school personnel. Proposed strategies might unfreeze traditional norms and procedures. On the other hand, Hispanic students could be better served by strategies that take into account their actual needs as determined by a thoughtful assessment process. Positive results would in turn lead to more satisfied students and indirectly to more satisfied teachers.

To increase the probability of successful implementation of desired programs, the following strategies are recommended:

- Enlist teachers, administrators, and community representatives to serve on an advisory committee that would be involved, beginning with the assessment phase.
- Present the data gathered in the assessment phase to various campus groups to receive their feedback and their ideas.
- Present the data to parent groups and ask for their feedback and their ideas.
- Present the overall plan to the school's principal and enlist his or her support.
- Encourage the district to employ an Hispanic counselor the next time an opening occurs.

A counselor wanting to increase the likelihood of success for a program designed to increase the leadership/school participation of Hispanic students could:

1. Invite the parents or guardians of the targeted students to an evening meeting, during which their children's potential is discussed and suggestions are made regarding how they can reinforce and encourage their children to assume leadership roles in the school.
2. Conduct a workshop for teachers of the targeted students and provide them with techniques for reinforcing and encouraging the leadership efforts of those students. The counselor could emphasize the following:
   a. The data collected by the counselor illustrating the degree to which Hispanic students are not participating in leadership positions in the school.
   b. Classroom interaction studies suggest that teachers often call on white students to answer questions and wait longer for their responses than for Hispanic students.
   c. Teachers can change the dynamics in their classrooms by changing their patterns of behavior toward their Hispanic students (i.e., call on them more often, allow them more time to respond, etc.).
   d. Teachers should reinforce efforts by the targeted Hispanic students to assume more active roles in the classroom and in the school.

Evaluating Programs Designed for Hispanic Students

Evaluation of efforts to meet the needs of Hispanic students can range from simple to complex, depending on the nature of the activities undertaken, the ease with which they lend themselves to observation and measurement, and the time available to the counselor. Evaluation strategies should reflect a systemic approach and consider the impact of the counselors' efforts on students *and* the counselor and counseling services, as well as other school personnel and school services and procedures. Several examples of simpler methods include:

- After implementing a program on alternative discipline strategies, count the number of Hispanic students referred to the administration for disciplinary purposes and compare with baseline data.

- After implementation of a series of group counseling sessions designed for Hispanic at-risk students, compare the dropout rate of participants with the school's Hispanic student dropout rate.
- After conducting a workshop on issues regarding the identification of Hispanic gifted students, determine the referral and selection rate for gifted and talented programs. Compare that rate with the previous year's rate of referral and selection.

Counselors needing more complex evaluation methods can:

- Administer pre- and postself-concept scales to Hispanic students participating in group counseling sessions.
- Administer pre- and postsurveys to teachers participating in a cultural awareness workshop on their knowledge of the school's Hispanic student population (number, SES characteristics, cultural traits).
- Determine the percent of Hispanic students mastering career search skills after participating in career search sessions.

The following case study highlights many of the points that have been discussed in this chapter.

CASE STUDY

Daniel

Daniel is an 8-year-old second-grader. He and his family arrived in the United States from Mexico two years ago. Daniel has a 14-year-old brother, Julian, who is in middle school. Julian fills a role that is common for children in recently immigrated families, serving as the family's link to the English-speaking world through his ability to translate. Three additional siblings born between Daniel and his brother are still in Mexico. The family's support system includes the father's brothers and their wives, all recent immigrants from Mexico. Daniel's father is a construction worker, and his mother is a housewife.

Daniel's academic performance has been average. He has consistently submitted required assignments, he has perfect attendance, and his interactions with teachers and peers have been good. Recently, Daniel's academic performance has declined, and he has become withdrawn. His teacher, Mrs. Strickland, noted that Daniel has failed several tests, that he has not had his parents sign the required school folder (which includes the tests he failed), and that he has not had his parents sign permission slips needed for planned field trips. As a result, Daniel has lost recess privileges, he has had to eat by himself at lunch time, and has not been allowed to participate in two field trips. (Although he had earned the right to participate in the field trips, the fact that he did not have written parental permission prevented him from doing so.)

Mrs. Strickland wrote the parents a note on Daniel's folder, explaining that they needed to sign his folder and that Daniel needed to study for his tests. She also telephoned Daniel's home and talked to "someone" there about the situation who said, "OK." Mrs. Strickland had become extremely frustrated because there had been no change. Every morning, she reprimanded Daniel for not bringing the required signed folder and demanded an explanation. Daniel did not respond.

Mrs. Strickland referred Daniel to the school counselor, who interviewed Daniel about the situation. A few minutes into the interview, the counselor asked how Daniel's parents were doing. Daniel responded that his mother was in Mexico because her mother had died, and she had gone to Mexico to attend the funeral. She had taken Julian with her, and Daniel was staying with his father at night and with one of his aunts in the afternoons.

After her interview with Daniel, the counselor met with Mrs. Strickland to help her understand what had been happening to Daniel. The counselor explained that Daniel's mother had been gone for two weeks and why. Mrs. Strickland could not understand why Daniel's mother would leave him for that period of time for a funeral. The counselor explained that Daniel had three siblings still living in Mexico who Daniel's mother had not seen for some time. In addition, she explained that the mourning period in Hispanic countries tends to extend over several weeks, so it was not unusual for Daniel's mother to be away for the time that she was. Mrs. Strickland still did not appear to understand, so the counselor moved on.

The counselor indicated to Mrs. Strickland that Daniel had become withdrawn because he missed his mother. She also told

Mrs. Strickland that his apparent noncompliance was related to the fact that his mother and Julian, who were responsible for communication with the school, had not been available for signing the school folder and field trip permission forms. In addition, because Daniel's mother had taken Julian, the "family translator," with her to Mexico, Mrs. Strickland had spoken to one of Daniel's aunts when she called on the telephone—an aunt who speaks very little English. The notes she sent home via Daniel's folder could not be read by any of Daniel's non-English-reading relatives.

The counselor proposed several interventions to Mrs. Strickland. First, she suggested that communication with the family should occur through a bilingual teacher's aide. She also suggested that Mrs. Strickland talk to Daniel more positively, acknowledge his feelings, and reinforce him for bringing in his signed folders and related materials. The counselor also arranged for Daniel to receive tutoring from one of the school's senior citizen volunteers.

Finally, the counselor and Daniel agreed to meet daily until Daniel's mother returned. The initial sessions focused on Daniel's feelings about his current family situation (including his grandmother's death, his mother and brother being gone) and his relationship with Mrs. Strickland. The counselor and Daniel developed specific strategies for getting folders and papers signed, for completing assignments, and for reacting to Mrs. Strickland.

CONCLUSION

The development of effective school counseling programs for Hispanic children and youth is critical, given the increasing Hispanic population in the schools and given the special problems faced by Hispanic students. School counselors should develop programs based on a systemic perspective that takes into account the social, economic, and political context within which Hispanic children and youth live and learn. Concurrently, school counselors should apply systematic procedures for assessing the characteristics and needs of their Hispanic clientele, and for planning, developing, and evaluating programs responsive to those characteristics and needs.

REFERENCES

Arredondo, P. (1991). Counseling Latinas. In C. C. Lee & B. L. Richardson (Eds.), *Multicultural issues in counseling: New approaches to diversity* (pp. 143–157). Alexandria, VA: American Association for Counseling and Development.

Ascher, C. (1985). *Raising Hispanic achievement*. New York: Columbia University, Institute for Urban and Minority Education. (ERIC Document Reproduction Service No. ED 256 842).

Baron, A., Jr. (1991). Counseling chicano college students. In C. C. Lee & B. L. Richardson (Eds.), *Multicultural issues in counseling: New approaches to diversity* (pp. 171–184). Alexandria, VA: American Association for Counseling and Development.

Barreto, J. (1986). *Puerto Ricans: Growing problems for a growing population*. Washington, DC: National Committee for Full Employment. (ERIC Document Reproduction Service No. ED 273 739).

Carrasquillo, A. L. (1991). *Hispanic children & youth in the United States: A resource guide*. New York: Garland Publishing.

Chahin, J. (1983). *Educational and occupational orientations of young Hispanic women in the Brownsville, Texas area*. (ERIC Document Reproduction Service No. ED 230 240).

Cottone, R. R. (1991). Counselor roles according to two counseling world views. *Journal of Counseling and Development, 69* (5), 398–401.

del Pinal, J. H., & DeNavas, C. (1990). *The Hispanic population in the United States: March 1989* (Series P-20, No. 444). Washington, DC: U.S. Department of Commerce.

Fernandez, F. (1989). *Five cities high school dropout study: Characteristics of Hispanic high school students*. Washington, DC: Aspira Association Inc. (ERIC Document Reproduction Service No. ED 322 240).

Garza, R. T., & Ames, R. E. (1974). A comparison of Anglo and Mexican-American college students on locus of control. *Journal of Consulting and Clinical Psychology, 42,* 919.

Garza, R. T., & Gallegos, P. I. (1985). Environmental influences and personal choice: A humanistic perspective on acculturation. *Hispanic Journal of Behavioral Sciences, 7* (4), 365–379.

Gonzalez, G. M. (1991). Cuban Americans: Counseling and human development issues, problems & approaches. In C. C. Lee & B. L. Richardson (Eds.), *Multicultural issues in counseling: New approaches to diversity* (pp. 157–171). Alexandria, VA: American Association for Counseling.

Gysbers, N. C., & Henderson, H. (1988). *Developing & managing your school guidance program*. Alexandria, VA: American Association for Counseling and Development.

Hartzler, K., & Franco, J. N. (1985). Ethnicity, division of household tasks and equity in marital roles: A comparison of Anglo and Mexican American couples. *Hispanic Journal of Behavioral Sciences, 7* (4), 333–344.

Hispanic Research Center. (1991). *Background and demand for engineering training and need for professional engineers in South Texas.* San Antonio: University of Texas.

Martinez, R., & Dukes, R. L. (1987). Race, gender and self-esteem among youth. *Hispanic Journal of Behavioral Sciences, 9* (4), 427–443.

Moore, H. A. (1988). Effects of gender, ethnicity, and school equity on students' leadership behaviors in a group game. *The Elementary School Journal, 88* (5), 515–526.

Orum, L. S. (1986). *The education of Hispanics: Status and implications.* Washington, DC: National Council of La Raza.

Pallas, A. M. (1988). School climate in American high schools, *Teachers College Record, 89* (4), 541–554.

Pederson, P. (1988). *A handbook for developing multicultural awareness.* Alexandria, VA: American Association for Counseling and Development.

Sabogal, F., Marin, G., Otero-Sabogal, R., VanOss, B., & Perez-Stable, E. J. (1987). Hispanic familism and acculturation: What changes and what doesn't? *Hispanic Journal of Behavioral Science, 9,* 397–412.

Schinke, S. P., Moncher, M. S., Palleja, J., Zayas, L. H., & Schilling, R. F. (1988). Hispanic youth, substance abuse, and stress: Implications for prevention research. *The International Journal of the Addictions, 23* (8), 809–826.

Shorr, D. N., & Young, T. W. (1984, April). *Locus of control: Ethnicity, SES, and academic achievement.* Paper presented at the American Educational Research Association annual meeting at New Orleans, LA. (ERIC Document Reproduction Service No. ED 254 939).

Strodl, P. (1988). *Ethnic differences in dealing with experiments in multiethnic middle schools.* Paper presented at the Urban Educational Research Conference, Brooklyn, NY, April 15. (ERIC Document Reproduction Service No. ED 297 044).

U.S. Department of Education. (1987). *1986 elementary and secondary school civil rights survey.* Washington DC. (ERIC Document Reproduction Service No. ED 304 485).

U.S. Department of Education. (1988). *Youth indicators 1988: Trends in the well-being of American youth.* Washington DC: Office of Educational Research and Improvement.

Velez, W. (1989). High school attrition among Hispanic and non-Hispanic White youth. *Sociology of Education, 62,* 119–133.

Zapata, J. T. (1990). [Corporal punishment as related to Hispanic student percentage]. Unpublished raw data.

Zavaleta, A. N. (1981). Variations in Hispanic health status. *Hispanic Research Center: Research Bulletin, 4,* 1–10. (ERIC Document Reproduction Service No. ED 229 464).

ADDITIONAL RESOURCES FOR COUNSELING WITH HISPANIC STUDENTS

Callejas, J. J. (1985). *The career guidance and counseling of in-school Hispanics: Some practical theoretical considerations.* Paper presented at the Annual Conference of the American Vocational Association, Atlanta, GA, December 6–10. (ERIC Document Reproduction Service No. 265 269).

Garcia, F., & Ybarra-Garcia, M. (1988). *Strategies for counseling Hispanics: Effects of racial and cultural stereotypes.* Olympia: Washington Office of the State Superintendent of Public Instruction. (ERIC Document Reproduction Service No. 300 687).

Grossman, H. (1984). *Educating Hispanic students.* Springfield, IL: Charles C. Thomas.

Lyons, J. J. (1989). *Legal responsibilities in education agencies serving national origin language minority student.* Washington, DC: The American University.

6

COUNSELING NATIVE AMERICAN STUDENTS

TIMOTHY C. THOMASON

INTRODUCTION

Although the continent of North America has been populated by Indian peoples for thousands of years, they are not at present a highly visible presence in much of the country. The 1990 census showed that the population of indigenous Americans is slightly under two million people, or less than 1 percent of the total population. Regardless of their numbers, Native Americans constitute a significant cultural group with very different values, problems, and resources, as compared to the general population. An understanding of these differences can assist school counselors in meeting the special needs of Indian students.

One of the main obstacles to understanding Native Americans is the myth of homogeneity—the idea that all Indians are similar. Actually, Indian people are incredibly diverse in their lifestyles, family structures, customs, and even languages. According to the Bureau of Indian Affairs (1988), there are 505 federally recognized tribes, 304 federal Indian reservations, and 250 different Indian languages. Over half of Native Americans live in urban areas (Fixico, 1986), and most large cities have at least 10,000 Indian residents (Stock, 1987). Thus, it is likely that there are at least some Indian students in many schools in the United States.

Given the diversity of Native American peoples, it is necessary to avoid the danger of stereotyping by recognizing the uniqueness of each individual. Some Native Americans have very traditional values, whereas others attempt to blend traditional customs with contemporary American culture. Indian students who do not look stereotypically Indian may easily be misidentified (Trimble, 1976). Adolescents want to fit in at school, and Native American students may appear anglicized from their outward appearance while remaining more traditional internally (Mahan & Criger, 1979). Since it is impossible for any one person to be an expert about all Indian tribes, a good approach is simply to accept each student as a unique individual and to exhibit a willingness to learn from each student.

EDUCATIONAL ISSUES FOR NATIVE AMERICAN YOUTH

Since their first contact with Europeans over 500 years ago, Native Americans have suffered from the effects of racial discrimination. In the past 100 years, a variety of social problems have developed, including poverty, unemployment, substandard housing, inadequate health care, and alcoholism. In addition, it has long been common practice for the U.S. government to separate Indian children from their families and place them in non-Indian foster homes or boarding homes, resulting in dysfunctional families (Herring, 1989, 1991).

As a result of facing so many challenges, it is hardly surprising that the academic achievement of many Indian children has suffered. As a group, their level of academic achievement is generally below that of the national average, although there is no reason to think they differ from other groups with respect to intellectual capacity. Indian children tend to score below their grade level on standardized tests and, by the completion of the twelfth grade, they are three grade levels below the national average (Dillard, 1983). Of course, some Indian children perform above grade level, thus the performance of any one student cannot be predicted in advance based on ethnicity.

In addition to the normal identity crises that all young people face, Native American children and teenagers often experience pressure to ignore their traditional values and assimilate into American culture. A student's family may emphasize the importance of traditional values, whereas at school teachers and peers consciously and/or unconsciously reinforce adherence to the values of mainstream society. This conflict can result in feelings of low self-worth, frustration, alienation, and a sense of hopelessness (Saslow & Harrover, 1979).

The stereotypical description of Native American students is that they are quiet, passive, withdrawn, and unexpressive (Trimble & LaFromboise, 1985; Mahan & Criger, 1979). While these adjectives may describe the behavior of some Indian students in interactions with some non-Indians, they are not typical of all Indian students. Also, it is important to remember that all people behave differently, depending on the situation. Quietness can be a sign of respect, and passivity can indicate receptivity to learning from others. In other words, all personality traits can be seen as being positive in some situations and negative in others. In a classroom situation where assertiveness, competitiveness, and highly verbal interaction are valued, some Indian students who have traditional values and upbringing may be at a disadvantage.

ISSUES IN COUNSELING NATIVE AMERICAN STUDENTS

The school counselor who works with Indian students may benefit by rethinking the nature of counseling. If the goal of counseling is to help students meet their needs, then intense verbal interaction about personal problems may be unnecessary. The counselor should avoid preconceptions about what an individual student needs. Before providing counseling services to any subset of students, including Native American students, some kind of needs assessment should be conducted. Many students will not have a clear understanding of what counseling is or how it can help. One way to orient students to counseling and to learn about their problems and needs at the same time is to have informal conversations in social situations. Some school counselors set up a drop-in center, which is basically a room where students can socialize with other students, have access to magazines, career information, and possibly refreshments, and talk with the counselor informally. Much valuable help can be provided to Indian students by making suggestions and providing advice within a social context.

It is important that school counselors be very open and available to Indian students, rather than assuming that students who need help will make an appointment for counseling. Few Indian students who are reared traditionally will seek out a stranger to discuss personal problems. They are more likely to respond well to a counselor who is sensitive to their needs and culture and is available for informal conversations. Indian students usually appreciate the counselor's interest in their home life, tribe, and so on, but intrusive and direct questioning should be avoided, particularly on the subjects of religion, tribal ceremonies, and tribal politics. The counselor should be seen as a source of information, wisdom, and concrete help for students, rather than as a disciplinarian or the person seen when one is in trouble.

Individual counseling is probably not the best format for meeting the needs of most Indian students (Dauphinais, LaFromboise, & Rowe, 1980), although those who have little identification with traditional Indian values may benefit from it as much as anyone else. If individual counseling is attempted, the counselor should be careful to go slowly and to be tolerant, open minded, patient, and accepting of silence (Youngman & Sadongei, 1974). Since counseling, by its very nature, tends to be primarily verbal, some Indian students may feel uncomfortable if pressured by a counselor to self-disclose personal concerns. The goal is not necessarily to get Indian students to talk, but to allow them the freedom to talk or not talk, as they wish. The counselor can adapt traditional counseling approaches so that they are less reliant on verbal interaction but are still responsive to students' needs. The counselor should take a gentle, noninvasive approach, avoid direct questions, and focus on building an atmosphere of acceptance so that an Indian student will feel comfortable.

Before bringing up a personal concern, an Indian student might test the counselor's trustworthiness and sincerity by requesting some kind of concrete assistance. Such requests should be responded to if at all possible; otherwise, the student might conclude that the counselor is not really interested in the student or capable of helping. Students may need help negotiating requirements of the school bureaucracy. For instance, some students who live near reservations may need to be absent from school to attend tribal ceremonies or to assist their family. Indian students often have many demands placed on them by relatives. These expectations are seen as part of being in a strong and stable family. This family stability should be encouraged.

The theoretical approach to take in counseling with Indian students is debatable, since no outcome studies have been conducted with this cultural group. It is quite possible that no theoretical model developed by Anglos for use with other Anglos will be appropriate for use with Native Americans. No one model of counseling is clearly superior to any other for use with this population (Thomason, 1991). Some general suggestions can be made, however, if they are understood as general guidelines rather than rules. The first step is to meet the Indian student as an individual and build rapport, patiently and without intrusive questioning. Subtly matching the client's nonverbal and paralinguistic behavior can help establish rapport and minimize the likelihood of offending the student in any way. Humor, self-disclosure, and warmth can also be helpful in establishing a trusting relationship with Indian students. The student should be allowed to control the pace and, to a degree, even the content of the conversation. A practical problem-solving approach to the student's concern is usually more helpful than a strictly psychodynamic, client-centered, behavioral, or cognitive approach. If the student asks for concrete assistance with practical problems, even outside the school setting, such assistance should be provided, if possible. The counselor should be the student's advocate in terms of helping him or her cope with problems related to fellow students, teachers, or school administrators.

Family counseling for Native American students is often more helpful than individual counseling and should be used whenever possible. In many Indian tribes, the individual's family extends to include aunts, uncles, and grandparents. The strength of family counseling with Indian students is that the family is likely to have far more influence over the student than the counselor or other school representatives. In addition, the family can provide the student with strength and support, which may not be readily available to the student in the school environment.

A related approach is tribal network therapy, which was developed by Attneave and Speck (Attneave, 1969; LaFromboise & Fleming, 1990; Speck & Attneave, 1973). In this approach, as many as 40 people—who are related to the client by blood, friendship, need, or proximity—are called together to provide support for the client. The goal is to build the coping skills of the client within the context of the group, both to resolve the current problem and improve the client's ability to handle future problems. This approach makes clear that problems exist in groups, rather than just in individuals, and the group is a powerful agent of change. Tribal network therapy builds a sense of community, facilitates creative problem solving, and helps ensure that benefits generalize beyond the identified client.

Peer counseling is also valuable and is likely to be utilized by Indian youth much more often than individual counseling. School counselors would be wise to set up peer counseling programs in their schools to promote such interaction. One should not assume, however, that any individual Indian student will automatically like another student who happens to be Indian. There is a degree of animosity between some tribes due to historical conflict, land disputes, and other cultural issues.

The school counselor can facilitate informal peer counseling by setting up mixers and other group situations where all students interested in meeting and talking with their peers about school and related matters can do so. It may also be helpful to set up a support group specifically for Indian students. Activity groups organized around a special interest, such as a sport or hobby, or a community or school project, bring students together in situations that promote informal peer counseling.

CASE STUDY

Sam

Sam was a 13-year-old Navajo boy in the eighth grade at a public school. He was quiet and well-behaved at school, but he was absent often, his grades were poor, and he usually appeared to be lonely and depressed. Although his performance scores on intelligence tests showed that he had slightly above-average ability, his achievement test scores in reading and math were two years below grade level. One of his teachers mentioned him to the school counselor, thinking that maybe Sam had a learning disability.

The school counselor read Sam's school records and learned that he had been struggling academically for several years. He had not been in much trouble except for missing school frequently, and twice he was sent home with his mother when he appeared to be intoxicated at school.

Resources

Many of the activities used in standard counseling groups can be used or adapted for use in groups for Native American students (Axelson, 1985; Dyer & Vriend, 1977; Morganett, 1990; Smith, 1977). There are also resources that describe how to conduct groups on specific topics that could be adapted for use with Native American students. For example, the book edited by Gerler, Hogan, and O'Rourke (1990) has chapters on groups for preventing drug abuse, improving academic achievement, career exploration, and identity development. A book edited by Blum (1990) has chapters on increasing career awareness, preventing substance abuse, and preventing dropouts. Atkinson, Morten, and Sue's (1989) Minority Identity Development Model is good background for conducting a group on Native American identity development. There are many good books, films, and videotapes about Native Americans, some of which are listed in the resource list at the end of this chapter.

CASE STUDY

Implementing a Counseling Program for Native American Students

Canyon Junior High School is located in a small city near the Navajo and Hopi reservations in southwestern United States. The newly hired school counselor, Mr. Miller, was non-Indian but was very interested in Indian cultures. He had taken a course on Indians of the Southwest at a local college and had participated in a cultural sensitivity workshop for educators sponsored by Navajo Community College. There were many Navajo and Hopi teenagers at the junior high school, but they rarely requested any counseling services, so Mr. Miller decided to implement a new approach to meet their potential counseling needs.

The counselor circulated a flyer to all students to announce that he would be available each school day for students who wanted to drop in and visit. The announcement made it clear that students could drop in just to talk or look at informational materials. The idea was to help students feel comfortable about stopping by even if they did not have a specific problem to discuss.

Mr. Miller put a couch and a coffee table in his office, some Indian art on the walls, and installed a small refrigerator stocked with soft drinks and juice. He put in a display rack of brochures and scriptographic booklets on common student concerns such as alcohol abuse, drug abuse, smoking, STDs, AIDS, stress, self-esteem, depression, and suicide. He also displayed informational materials on career planning, academic tutoring, school sports and extracurricular activities, and brochures from several social service agencies in the community.

Within a few days, students began to stop by. Rather than ask why they came by, Mr. Miller just welcomed them and invited them to sit down. He offered them something to drink and shared a bowl of peanuts. The students were surprised but receptive to the friendly overtures, and seemed relieved that they were not asked personal questions and could simply chat with the counselor about classes or school events or just look at the informational materials. If the students seemed intent on studying the materials, he let them sit in the office while he did paperwork at his desk. By his behavior, Mr. Miller conveyed the message that students were welcomed to stop by, even without a specific reason, and that he was available to talk with them about anything.

After a few weeks, various students became accustomed to dropping by the counselor's office. Often, they had no specific concern at the time, but some students would call the counselor later and make an appointment for a private counseling session. The Native American students usually came by in twos or threes. At first, they seemed shy and somewhat suspicious of the counselor's motives, but over time Mr. Miller earned their trust by responding to their requests for assistance.

For example, when a student complained about unfair treatment from a teacher, Mr. Miller volunteered to talk to the teacher to help resolve the conflict. Another Indian student said she was penalized for missing two days of school to attend an important ceremony on the reservation. Mr. Miller met with the school principal to discuss whether this was discriminatory, since other students were allowed to miss school for religious reasons, and the policy was changed. Another Indian student complained about non-Indian students making racist comments toward the Indian students, so Mr. Miller got approval to hold a series of cultural sensitivity training sessions as a part of certain classes. He also arranged for films and videotapes on Native American themes to be shown at school occasionally for the entertainment and education of all the students.

The counselor was able to earn the trust of the Indian students because he showed a genuine interest in them as people. He was willing to experiment with new ways of relating to the students and provided practical assistance whenever needed. Once he gave a stranded student a ride home, and he visited the reservation occasionally to tour cultural centers, attend craft fairs and events, and visit students in their homes (when invited to do so). These activities demonstrated Mr. Miller's genuine interest in Indian culture and his willingness to learn about the historical, environmental, and cultural milieu of his students.

Mr. Miller was able to provide a great deal of informal counseling during the times when Indian students dropped by his office. Many of the students who never asked for a private session seemed satisfied by the informal assistance they received. Some of the students did request and received individual counseling. The counselor never insisted on seeing Native American students alone. Students were encouraged to bring friends or family members to the counseling sessions. Often, the family members spoke more than the students, but the counselor observed that the student listened carefully to everything that was said and seemed to benefit from the sessions even without talking a lot.

Mr. Miller also set up a mutual support group for Indian students that met weekly. The students worked on projects together, such as organizing an exhibit of Indian art at the school, writing articles on Indian issues for the school paper, and compiling a scrapbook of articles on successful contemporary Native Americans in the arts, business, education, and other professions. They also watched videotapes of movies on Indian themes, played music by Indian musicians, and read books by Indian authors and discussed them. The counselor served as the advisor for the group and invited Native American elders, teachers, and health and social workers to speak to the group on topics of interest. Through these activities, the students formed social relationships, improved their self-concept as Native Americans, and provided support for each other in dealing with problems.

The counselor was always available for assistance and support, but once the group was established, he backed off and let the students run it. Occasionally, he assessed their interests and needs by talking to them informally and suggested new activities for them to explore. For example, when several students expressed a concern about alcohol abuse affecting the lives of their friends and families, Mr. Miller started a counseling group on the subject. This group was run somewhat in the style of the traditional Indian "talking circle." The students sit in a circle and may talk or just listen. The speaker holds an object such as a feather, which is passed around, and only the person with the object can speak. Each person speaks as long as necessary, and each person speaks only for himself or herself, without directing questions to other group members. This encourages self-expression and empathic listening and discourages argumentativeness and defensiveness.

In the alcohol group, the students talked about the reasons people drink, the effects of alcohol on people they knew, and proposed criteria for the responsible use of alcohol. They also considered the negative social effects of alcohol abuse by Native Americans in general, and the need for Indian people to deal with and fight the common stereotype of the "drunken Indian" by not abusing alcohol. The group discussed alternative ways to respond to stress, including safe and legal traditional Native American methods to relax, achieve peace of mind, and experience spiritual harmony.

Another peer counseling/tutoring group was set up for Native American students who were performing below their academic potential. With the guidance of a tutor, the group members met weekly to review classroom work and to support and encourage each other to do their best. A career counseling group allowed students to learn more about their vocational aptitudes and interests and encouraged them to begin to think about career options. The discussion included an overview of job opportunities on the reservation as well as off the reservation. Another group specifically for Native American students focused on identity development and the conflict the students felt about being pulled between traditional Indian culture and values and contemporary American values.

The school sponsored several special activities for the Native American students over the course of several years. These included an annual Native American Day, an outdoor discovery weekend similar to those conducted by Outward Bound, a Vision Quest, and a sweat lodge experience. Although these activities were sponsored by the school, and Mr. Miller attended them as an advisor, the activities were conducted by Native American people with expertise and experience in each specific area.

In summary, throughout the school year, Mr. Miller used a wide variety of methods to meet the needs of the Native American students in his school. In addition to the drop-in model and individual counseling, the counselor utilized family counseling, peer counseling, traditional counseling groups, groups on specific issues, activity groups, discussion groups based on movies and books, and cross-cultural sensitivity training. This combination of traditional and innovative counseling methods was effective in showing the Native American students that both they and their cultures were highly valued. The students developed more positive self-concepts as Native Americans, worked through their specific problems, and improved their academic performance.

CONCLUSION

As a group, Native Americans have a long and fascinating history. As individuals, contemporary Native Americans face many challenges, but they also have many traditional cultural strengths from which to draw. Indian youth are in a difficult position, pulled as they often are between ancient values and the seductive fads and fashions of commercialized America, complete with sex, drugs, and MTV. School counselors who approach Native American students with open minds have a unique opportunity. They can help influence their choices and, in doing so, learn a great deal themselves.

REFERENCES

Atkinson, D. R., Morten, G., & Sue, D. W. (1989). *Counseling American minorities*. Dubuque, IA: William C. Brown.

Axelson, J. A. (1985). *Counseling and development in a multicultural society*. Monterey, CA: Brooks/Cole.

Attneave, C. (1969). Therapy in tribal settings and urban network intervention. *Family Process, 8,* 192–210.

Blum, D. J. S. (1990). *Group counseling for secondary schools*. Springfield, IL: Charles C. Thomas.

Bureau of Indian Affairs. (1988). *American Indians today*. Washington DC: Author.

Dauphinais, P., Dauphinais, L., & Rowe, W. (1981). Effects of race and communication style on Indian perceptions of counselor effectiveness. *Counselor Education and Supervision, 21,* 72–80.

Dauphinais, P., LaFromboise, T., & Rowe, W. (1980). Perceived problems and sources of help for American Indian students. *Counselor Education and Supervision, 20,* 37–44.

Dillard, J. M. (1983). *Multicultural counseling.* Chicago: Nelson-Hall.

Dyer, W. W., & Vriend, J. (1977). *Counseling techniques that work.* New York: Funk & Wagnalls.

Edwards, E. D., & Edwards, M. E. (1989). American Indians: Working with individuals and groups. In D. R. Atkinson, G. Morten, & D. W. Sue (Eds.), *Counseling American minorities* (pp. 72–84). Dubuque, IA: William C. Brown.

Fixico, D. L. (1986). *Termination and relocation: Federal Indian policy, 1945–1960.* Albuquerque: University of New Mexico Press.

Gerler, E. R., Hogan, C. C., & O'Rourke, K. (Eds.). (1990). *Challenge of counseling in middle schools.* Ann Arbor, MI: ERIC Counseling and Personnel Services Clearinghouse.

Herring, R. D. (1989). The American Native family: Dissolution by coercion. *Journal of Multicultural Counseling and Development, 17,* 4–13.

Herring, R. D. (1991). Counseling Native American youth. In C. C. Lee & B. L. Richardson (Eds.), *Multicultural issues in counseling: New approaches to diversity* (pp. 37–47). Alexandria, VA: American Association for Counseling and Development.

LaFromboise, T. D., & Fleming, C. (1990). Keeper of the fire: A profile of Carolyn Attneave. *Journal of Counseling & Development, 68,* 537–547.

Lewis, R., & Ho, M. (1989). Social work with Native Americans. In D. Atkinson, G. Morten, & D. Sue (Eds.), *Counseling American minorities* (pp. 51–58). Dubuque, IA: William C. Brown.

Mahan, J. M., & Criger, M. K. (1979). Culturally oriented instruction for Native American students. In G. Henderson (Ed.), *Understanding and counseling ethnic minorities* (pp. 318–328). Springfield, IL: Charles C. Thomas.

Morganett, R. S. (1990). *Skills for living: Group counseling activities for young adolescents.* Champaign, IL: Research Press.

Saslow, H. L., & Harrover, M. J. (1979). Research on psychosocial adjustment of Indian youth. In G. Henderson (Ed.), *Understanding and counseling ethnic minorities* (pp. 291–306). Springfield, IL: Charles C. Thomas.

Smith, M. (1977). *A practical guide to value clarification.* La Jolla, CA: University Associates.

Speck, R., & Attneave, C. (1973). *Family networks: Retribalization and healing.* New York: Random House.

Stock, L. (1987). Native Americans: A brief profile. *Journal of Visual Impairment and Blindness, 81,* 152.

Thomason, T. C. (1991). Counseling Native Americans: An introduction for non-Native American counselors. *Journal of Counseling and Development, 69,* 321–327.

Trimble, J. E. (1976). Value differences among American Indians: Concerns for the concerned counselor. In P. Pedersen, W. J. Lonner, & J. G. Draguns (Eds.), *Counseling across cultures* (pp. 65–81). Honolulu: University Press of Hawaii.

Trimble, J. E., & LaFromboise, T. D. (1985). American Indians and the counseling process: Culture, adaptation, and style. In P. Pedersen (Ed.), *Handbook of cross-cultural counseling and therapy* (pp. 127–134). Westport, CT: Greenwood Press.

Youngman, G., & Sadongei, M. (1974). Counseling the American Indian child. *Elementary School Guidance and Counseling, 8*, 273–277.

ADDITIONAL RESOURCES FOR COUNSELING WITH NATIVE AMERICAN STUDENTS

Ambrosino, M. (Producer). (1990). *Myths and moundbuilders* [Videotape]. Beverly Hills, CA: Pacific Arts Video Publishing.

Attneave, C. (1982). American Indians and Alaska Native families: Emigrants in their own homeland. In M. McGoldrick, J. Pearce, & J. Giordano (Eds.), *Ethnicity and family therapy* (pp. 55–83). New York: Guilford.

Attneave, C. L. (1985). Practical counseling with American Indian and Alaska Native clients. In P. Pedersen (Ed.), *Handbook of cross-cultural counseling and therapy* (pp. 135–140). Westport, CT: Greenwood Press.

Brown, D. (1970). *Bury my heart at Wounded Knee.* New York: Holt, Rinehart and Winston.

Bryde, J. F. (1971). *Indian students and guidance.* Boston: Houghton Mifflin.

Coughlin, D. (Producer). (1981). *Right of ways* [Videotape]. Tempe: KAET.

Cross, S. (Producer). (1982). *Walking in a sacred manner* [Motion Picture]. Chicago: International Film Bureau.

Dinges, N. G., Trimble, J. E., Manson, S. M., & Pasquale, F. L. (1981). Counseling and psychotherapy with American Indians and Alaskan Native. In A. J. Marsella & P. B. Pedersen (Eds.), *Cross-cultural counseling and psychotherapy* (pp. 243–276). New York: Pergamon.

Ehle, J. (1988). *Trail of tears.* New York: Doubleday.

Hammerschlag, C. A. (1988). *The dancing healers.* San Francisco: Harper and Row.

Harrar, L. (Producer.) (1984). *Make my people live* [Motion Picture]. New York: Time Life Video.

Heinrich, R. K., Corbine, J. L., & Thomas, K. R. (1990). Counseling Native Americans. *Journal of Counseling & Development, 69,* 128–133.

LaFromboise, T. D. (1988). American Indian mental health policy. *American Psychologist, 43,* 388–397.

LaFromboise, T. D., Trimble, J. E., & Mohatt, G. V. (1990). Counseling intervention and American Indian tradition: An integrative approach. *Counseling Psychologist, 18,* 628–654.

Lesiak, C. (Producer.) (1986). *White man's way* [Videotape]. Lincoln, NE: Great Plains National Instructional Television.

Lucas, P. (Producer). (1986). *The honour of all: The story of Alkalai Lake* [Videotape]. Alkalai Lake, B.C., Canada: Phil Lucas Productions.

Manson, S. M., & Trimble, J. E. (1982). American Indian and Alaska Native communities. In L. R. Snowden (Ed.), *Reaching the underserved* (pp. 143–163). Beverly Hills, CA: Sage.

McWhirter, J. J., & Ryan, C. A. (1991). Counseling the Navajo: Cultural understanding. *Journal of Multicultural Counseling and Development, 18,* 74–82.

Momaday, N. S. (1968). *House made of dawn.* New York: Harper and Row.

Neihardt, J. G. (1972). *Black Elk speaks.* Lincoln, NE: University of Nebraska Press.

Schmitz, A. (Producer). (1990). *Seasons of the Navajo* [Videotape]. Beverly Hills, CA: Pacific Arts Video Publishing.

Silko, L. M. (1977). *Ceremony.* New York: Viking Press.

Trimble, J. E., & Fleming, C. M. (1989). Providing counseling services for Native American Indians: Client, counselor, and community characteristics. In P. B. Pedersen, J. G. Draguns, W. J. Lonner, & J. E. Trimble (Eds.), *Counseling across culture* (3rd ed.) (pp. 177–204). Honolulu: University Press of Hawaii.

Trimble, J. E., & LaFromboise, T. (1985). American Indians and the counseling process: Culture, adaptation, and style. In P. Pedersen (Ed.), *Handbook of cross-cultural counseling and therapy.* Westport, CT: Greenwood Press.

Viola, H. J. (1990). *After Columbus: The Smithsonian chronicle of the North American Indians.* Washington, DC: Smithsonian Books.

Waldman, C. (1985). *Atlas of the North American Indian.* New York: Facts on File Publications.

Weatherford, J. (1991). *Native roots.* New York: Crown Publishers.

PART III

CULTURALLY RESPONSIVE SCHOOL CONSULTATION, CLASSROOM GUIDANCE, COORDINATION, AND ACCOUNTABILITY

Consultation is a helping process that provides indirect services to students. It involves remedial or developmental problem solving with important individuals who have a stake in students' education. Consultation helps to empower these individuals to work more effectively with students. *Classroom guidance* is a helping process consisting of organized activities that are generally delivered to students in classrooms during the elementary school years. These activities focus on the development of personal/social understanding and skills. *Coordination* is a helping process where a counselor brings together resources in the school and the community to maximize student development. *Accountability* refers to the process of gathering information to assess student needs and evaluate counseling effectiveness. The chapters that comprise this part of the book provide direction on how to carry out these important counselor functions in culturally diverse school settings.

7

CROSS-CULTURAL SCHOOL CONSULTATION

CAROL F. DUNCAN

The interest in consultation as a service delivery approach in the schools has undoubtedly been one of the most significant developments within the past 25 years (Medway, 1982). Many surveys indicate that helping professionals in the schools view consultation as one of the most preferred job functions (Barbanel & Hoffenburg-Rutman, 1974; Cook & Patterson, 1977; Manley & Manley, 1978; Meacham & Peckham, 1978), and teachers as well as other educational personnel rate consultation as among the most important services that counseling professionals bring to the school (Bardon, 1976; Curtis & Zins, 1981; Gutkin, 1980). Certainly, the influence of shrinking federal resources, as well as changes in school organizational practices (e.g., team decision making vs. individual professional responsibility), has contributed to this growing interest. The pragmatic and conceptual merits of consultation as an indirect service approach in a time of nonexpanding resources is attractive (Pryzwansky, 1986).

This chapter explores theory related to cross-cultural consultation and introduces strategies for the delivery of consultation services to culturally diverse populations. The purpose of this chapter is threefold. First, the definition of consultation as a service delivery approach in the schools will be explored. Second, the impact of race/ethnicity as a variable in the process and outcome of consultation will be discussed. Third, strategies for working with culturally diverse teachers, students, and parents in the consultation process will be delineated.

CONSULTATION DEFINED

An adequate and comprehensive definition of consultation has eluded theorists and researchers in the area of consultation for years. Mannino and Shore (1985) have recently indicated that confusion surrounding the definition of consultation has restricted advancement in the area, while others indicate that the definitional confusion surrounding consultation is not unlike confusion noted in other areas—for example, counseling or psychotherapy, in which practitioners and researchers operate from many different theoretical viewpoints (Brown, Pryzwansky, & Schulte, 1987).

Given that this chapter will focus on consultation as a service delivery approach to teachers and parents, the definition provided by Brown, Pryzwansky, and Schulte (1987) will be adopted:

> Consultation is defined as a voluntary problem-solving process that can be initiated and terminated by either the consultant [school counselor] or consultee [teacher or parent]. It is engaged in primarily for the purpose of assisting consultees to develop attitudes and skills that will enable them to function more effectively with an individual, group, or organization for which they have responsibility. Thus, the goals are two-fold: enhancing services to third parties, and improving the abilities of consultees to function in areas of concern to them. (p. 8)

CROSS-CULTURAL CONSULTATION DEFINED

In this chapter, cross-cultural consultation is defined as a consultation relationship in which two or more of the participants differ with respect to ethnic or cultural background. These differences may include, but are not limited to, ethnic/racial differences in values, attitudes, language or behavior. Westermeyer and Hausman (1974) provided four scenarios for understanding the possible ethnic combinations that may occur in a consultative relationship.

The paradigm for the first scenario occurs when an ethnic minority individual is the client (i.e., student), and the consultant (i.e., school counselor) and consultee (i.e., teacher or other educational professional) are members of the predominant European American cultural group. The second scenario represents the case in which the consultant is a member of the predominant cultural group and the consultee and client are minority group members. Scenario three represents a paradigm in which the consultant and client are of a minority group and the consultee is of the predominant cultural group. The last scenario represents a case in which all three parties—the consultant, consultee, and client—differ in racial/ethnic background.

Although there are many instances in which cross-cultural consultation can occur (e.g., consulting with or about foreign students, consulting in a foreign country, consultation relationships in which a European American person is the consultee), this chapter will be limited to situations in which the counseling professional, as consultant, is a member of the predominant European American cultural group and the consultee or client is a member of an ethnic minority cultural group. The ideas and concepts presented in the chapter, however, are important to all, regardless of ethnic/racial background.

CULTURAL DIFFERENCES IN THE CONSULTATION PROCESS

The need to focus on cultural differences in the consultation process is underscored by research in the counseling literature suggesting that ethnic minority clients terminate counseling contacts (after the initial session) to a significantly greater degree than do European American clients. Furthermore, ethnic minority clients frequently report feeling misunderstood by European American helping professionals (Sue, 1990).

Relationship building at the entry stage of any helping relationship has been a recurrent theme in the literature (Dinkmeyer & Dinkmeyer, 1976; Gutkin & Curtis, 1982; Parsons & Meyers, 1984; Raffaniello, 1981; Westwood & Ishiyama, 1990). Several theorists have suggested that the consultant's demonstrated cultural awareness at the entry stage of the helping relationship is seen as a significant factor affecting the process and outcome of cross-cultural interactions (Banks, 1988; Gibbs, 1980, 1985; LaFromboise, 1992; Sue, 1990).

The entry phase of consultation can be described as the "process whereby the consultant comes into contact with, establishes a working relationship with, and begins the analysis of problems presented [by the consultee]" (Pipes, 1981, p. 11). The entry phase is a dynamic process in that the consultant is obtaining information about the consultee's concerns, while the consultee is gathering information about the consultant's style of relating, communicating, and problem solving.

While cross-cultural counseling research has focused on a variety of ethnic combinations in the literature, there is a dearth of research regarding cross-cultural consultation. Gibbs (1980, 1985) has been most prolific in exploring cross-cultural consultation. Her work has focused on the interactions between African Americans and European Americans in cross-cultural consultation. Based on data from sociological research, Gibbs has suggested that African American consultees place a higher value on the consultant's interpersonal skills as opposed to the consultant's instrumental or task-related skills at the entry phase of consultation. She formulated three propositions regarding cultural differences between African American and European American consultees in consultation: "(a) there are ethnic differences in the initial orientation to the consultant-consultee relationship, (b) these differences are along the lines of interpersonal versus instrumental competence, and (c) these differences have significant implications for the implementation of the consultation process and its outcome" (Gibbs, 1980, p. 195).

Gibbs has contended that African American consultees believe that they must feel a degree of trust and interpersonal comfortableness with the consultant before they can effectively engage in the problem-solving process of consultation. Using psychological ethnological studies, she outlined a sequence of five stages that exemplified the interactions between the European American consultant and the African American consultee at the entry phase of consultation. In this model, Gibbs defined *interpersonal orientation* as the ability of the consultant to evoke positive attitudes toward him or her and his or her actions by way of personal authenticity, genuineness, positive identification, and acceptance. *Instrumental orientation* is defined as the degree of effectiveness with which a goal or task is accomplished. A brief description of the model follows.

Stage I: Appraisal Stage

This is the initial stage of contact between the consultant (counselor) and consultee (teacher/parent). During this stage, the ethnic minority consultee "sizes up" the consultant in terms of the consultant's ability to be genuine and approachable. Typically, the consultee is aloof and guarded, or superficially pleasant, and may harbor feelings of suspiciousness, distrust, and hostility toward the consultant. European American consultees, on the other hand, are evaluating the overall consultation project and the professional skills of the consultant on entering the system.

Stage II: Investigation Stage

Stage II follows closely behind the initial "sizing up" stage and is characterized by the ethnic minority consultee's attempt to challenge the consultant concerning his or her background qualifications, values, and opinions. This is an attempt to place the consultant along some ideological spectrum in terms of previous work with minority clients as well as ability to equalize differences between himself or herself and the consultee. European American consultees, on the other hand, will inquire about details of the project, not about the consultant's personal characteristics and values.

Stage III: Involvement Stage

Stage III only follows if the ethnic minority consultee has evaluated the consultant favorably. If the consultee has positively identified with the consultant based on the previous "checking out" periods, the consultee will begin to open up and self-disclose. An attempt to establish a more personal relationship with the consultant may occur at this stage based on perceived mutuality and similarity—for example, sharing personal information or inviting the consultant to lunch or coffee or to an ethnic community activity. If the consultant has not "checked out" previously, he or she may find further effects doomed to failure. European American consultees will continue the relationship on a professional level.

Stage IV: Commitment Stage

Stage IV follows only if the consultant responds flexibly and sensitively to the efforts of the ethnic minority consultee to establish a more personal relationship. The consultee will become committed to the professional relationship. However, the commitment will be in terms of loyalty and personal regard, rather than belief in the effectiveness of the consultation experience. European American consultees will be committed to the goals of the project.

Stage V: Engagement Stage

Both ethnic minority and European American consultees will make a final commitment to the goals established. However, European American consultees will make their commitment in terms of the consultant's demonstrated instrumental competence and ethnic minority consultees will make their commitment based on the consultant's demonstrated interpersonal skills.

An example that illustrates Gibbs's theoretical model is described in the following scenario:

> A school counselor attending a school-based committee meeting was informed that a fifth-grade teacher had requested assistance with a student exhibiting disruptive behavior in the classroom. In this case, the counselor (consultant) was a majority group member (European American), and both the teacher (consultee) and student (client) were African American. The counselor was new to the school and had not met the teacher. She was informed that the teacher was hesitant to refer the student for consideration of special school services and had asked for assistance in developing alternative teaching and behavioral management techniques to help the child succeed in the classroom. The counselor initially attempted to contact the teacher by leaving a note in the teacher's mailbox. When the teacher did not respond to the notes, the counselor initiated a direct contact, introducing herself and offering her assistance in developing the alternative plan. At this contact, the teacher appeared somewhat curt *(Appraisal Stage)*. She indicated she did not have time to discuss the student and was not forthcoming with future times to meet. The counselor dropped by the teacher's classroom the following week and, at that time, the teacher suggested meeting in the teachers' lounge during the next day's lunch period. She appeared reserved and did not disclose her concerns about the student.
>
> The next day, the school counselor arrived at the lounge to find several teachers enjoying lunch together, including the consultee. All of the teachers were minority group members. The counselor joined the group for lunch. She was not verbally recog-

nized by the consultee and no discussion of the client took place. Over a five-day period, the counselor was increasingly welcomed and incorporated into the group's conversation during this lunch time *(Investigation Stage)*. The conversation included discussion about local governmental politics, the recent L.A. riots, and opinions about the increasing political activism by minority students at the local (predominantly European American) university. The counselor's opinions were asked for and reflected upon along with other group members. After the first week of these lunch gatherings, the consultee stated to the group that she had been "dragging her feet" in relation to working with the school counselor and then excused herself and the counselor so they could "do some work" *(Commitment/Engagement Stage)*.

This scenario illustrates the stage-based process that is characteristic of cross-cultural consultations for African Americans and European Americans, as outlined by Gibbs. This interaction suggests that the teacher (consultee) evaluated the counselor (consultant) from an interpersonal orientation that was based on the counselor's ability to evoke feelings of trust, genuineness, and equalitarianism. Once the counselor was viewed favorably by the teacher on these dimensions, the teacher was ready to focus on the task at hand.

This model illustrates the impact of cultural differences in cross-cultural consultation. However, one cannot assume Gibbs's model can be generalized across cultural groups. For example, cross-cultural counseling research suggests that an inverse process may be most effective in working with a member of the Asian-American minority group (Sue, 1990).

CROSS-CULTURAL CONSULTATION STRATEGIES

Consulting with Ethnic Minority Group Teachers and Parents

Counseling professionals who plan to work cross culturally as consultants must develop the knowledge base necessary for interpreting cross-cultural interchanges accurately. This knowledge base should include but not be limited to (1) the possible influence of sociocultural differences between members of different cultural groups at the entry stage of consultation (as previously noted) and (2) an awareness of the concept of racial identity development and its potential impact on the cross-cultural interchange.

Racial identity development has been viewed as an important factor in affecting minority group members' preferences for counselor race. Theorists and researchers suggest that identity development, as a minority-group member, progresses through a series of stages that reflect the minority person's view of self, others in the same minority group, others of another minority group, and those in the majority group (Sue, 1990). Atkinson, Morten, and Sue (1989) have applied this theory to produce a model of minority identity development, which defines these stages along with corresponding attitudes and behaviors. Others have applied this theory to produce a model of European American identity development (Corvin & Wiggins, 1989; Hardiman, 1982; Helms, 1984; Sabnani & Ponterotto, 1991).

Awareness and application of these two concepts will work to alleviate mistakes and misinterpretation that might lead to premature termination of the consultation interchange. Furthermore, the consultant will be better equipped to modify his or her approach so to better fit the needs and expectations of the consultee.

Utilizing the concept of minority identity development, four scenarios follow that might represent a cross-cultural interchange with a minority consultee (teacher or parent) at each stage of minority identify development. Culturally responsive strategies are suggested for each interchange.

Stage I: Conformity
A minority group member, whose world view is reflective of Stage I of minority identity development, thinks and acts in ways that are suggestive of a preference for the predominant (European American) cultural value system. A negative view of one's own culture is reflected. For example, a minority group parent at this stage might ask that his child be taught by a European American teacher—"European American teachers are smarter and have the best education." A response to this scenario might be to create dissonance for the parent by telling about minority group teachers within the school who have demonstrated effectiveness with majority and minority group students. Providing an opportunity for the parent to observe in the minority group teacher's classroom might be useful.

Stage II: Dissonance

A minority group person at Stage II begins to experience events that create dissonance with the predominant culture world view. A parent at this stage might begin to wonder aloud if his or her child is being negatively targeted by European American teachers due to minority group status. A culturally responsive strategy would be to accept the parent's view and to help clarify it by searching for validating or disconfirming evidence. Acceptance and exploration of negative feelings toward the majority group might be needed at this stage.

Stage III: Immersion

A minority group person at Stage III acts and thinks in ways that reflect "culturocentricism" and rejection of the majority group. At this stage, a minority group teacher might refuse to discuss a child with a European American consultant. One culturally responsive strategy would be to openly explore hostile feelings the consultee may have toward the consultant along ethnic/racial lines. Meeting the consultee on his or her own terms and/or being responsive to the possible request for a minority group consultant are other suggestions.

Stages IV and V: Interpretation and Awareness

A minority group member, at these stages, acts and thinks in ways that reflect selective appreciation across cultural groups. In this scenario, the minority group teacher explores the possibility of racial stereotyping as one hypothesis among several for a student's misbehavior. To be culturally responsive at this stage, the consultant must have a working knowledge of cultural differences in learning and behavior and be able to explore all hypotheses about the student behavior in an adequate manner.

Consultants as Advocates for Cross-Cultural Understanding: Macrolevel Consultation

Another consideration in cross-cultural interchanges involves the triad in which the identified client is an ethnic minority group student. The consultant can enhance the development of cultural sensitivity among all consultees by (1) increasing the consultee's (teacher and parent) awareness of the concept of minority identity development and its effect on students' interpersonal behavior and achievement, (2) increasing the consultee's awareness of sociocultural differences in learning styles and behavior, (3) increasing the consultee's awareness of systemic factors that impede progress for minority group students, and (4) facilitating professional development in the area of multicultural education and curriculum.

Both systemic and situationally specific strategies can be utilized to promote these objectives. At the systemic level, the consultant can utilize workshops and presentations (for teachers and parents) to share information about the concept of minority identity development and its impact (as well as the impact of other cultural variations) on learning, behavior, and communication. The consultant can utilize group consultations to promote multicultural curricular development. Utilizing an organizational consultation paradigm, the consultant can promote systemic change through research, evaluation, and exploration of policy and practice that might negatively impact minority students.

On a one-to-one level, the consultant can aid a consultee's understanding of the impact of a student's emerging minority identity and how that process might affect the student's behavior and learning. The consultant can provide information to the consultee regarding educational programming and materials that will promote a positive minority identity. The consultant can provide information, at the consultative level, about cultural variations in learning, verbal expression, and behavior to prevent misinterpretation of student behavior or academic achievement (Lee & Rotella, 1991). Individual consultation can also take place regarding issues related to multicultural curriculum development.

CONCLUSION

Although consultation is rated by school personnel as one of the most important services that counselors bring to the schools, little attention has been paid to the impact of cultural differences on the process and outcome of cross-cultural consultation interchanges. Consultants have largely been left to their own sensitivities regarding cultural differences when working with culturally diverse consultees. This chapter has attempted to address the dearth of literature in this area by offering some practical strategies for future cross-cultural consultation interchanges.

The premises of this chapter were threefold: (1) consultants must be aware of their own personal values and beliefs, (2) consultants must have an awareness of their current consultative style, and (3) consultants must adapt their style and views to fit the needs of the consultee in order for successful cross-cultural consultation to occur. A willingness to explore the possibility that cultural differences between the consultant and consultee may serve to impede the consultation interchange and an ability to address these issues by adapting the consultative style to fit the consultee's needs and expectations are both essential ingredients for successful cross-cultural consultation interchanges. By way of culturally diverse training and experiences, consultants can begin to develop the sensitivities necessary for these successful interchanges to occur.

REFERENCES

Atkinson, D. R., Morten, G., & Sue, D. W. (1989). A minority identity development model. In D. R. Atkinson, G. Morten, & D. W. Sue (Eds.), *Counseling American minorities* (pp. 35–52). Dubuque, IA: William C. Brown.

Banks, J. A. (1988). *Multicultural education: Theory and practice* (2nd ed.). Boston: Allyn and Bacon.

Barbanel, L., & Hoffenburg-Rutman, J. (1974). Attitudes toward job responsibilities and training satisfaction of school psychologists: A comparative study. *Psychology in the Schools, 11,* 424–429.

Bardon, J. (1976). The state of the art (and science) of school psychology. *American Psychologist, 31,* 785–791.

Brown, D., Pryzwansky, W. B., & Schulte, A. C. (1987). *Psychological consultation: Introduction to theory and practice.* Boston: Allyn and Bacon.

Cook, V. J., & Patterson, J. G. (1977). Psychologists in the schools of Nebraska: Professional functions. *Psychology in the Schools, 14,* 371–376.

Corvin, S., & Wiggins, F. (1989). An antiracism training model for White professionals. *Journal of Multicultural Counseling and Development, 17,* 105–114.

Curtis, M. J., & Zins, J. E. (1981). Consultative effectiveness as perceived by experts in consultation and classroom teachers. In M. J. Curtis & J. E. Zins (Eds.), *The theory and practice of school consultation* (pp. 88–96). Springfield, IL: Charles C. Thomas.

Dinkemeyer, D., & Dinkemeyer, F., Jr. (1976). Contributions of Adlerian psychology in school counseling interviews. *Psychology in the Schools, 13,* 32–38.

Gibbs, J. T. (1980). The interpersonal orientation in mental health consultation: Toward a model of ethnic variations in consultation. *The Journal of Community Psychology, 8,* 303–308.

Gibbs, J. T. (1985a). Treatment relationships with African American clients: Interpersonal vs. instrumental strategies. In G. Germain (Ed.), *Advances in clinical social work practice.* Silver Spring, MD: NASW, Inc.

Gibbs, J. T. (1985b). Can we continue to be color-blind and class-bound? *The Counseling Psychologist, 13,* 426–435.

Gutkin, T. B. (1980). Teacher perceptions of consultation services provided by school psychologists. *Professional Psychology, 11,* 637–642.

Gutkin, T. B., & Curtis, M. J. (1982). School-based consultation: Theory and techniques. In C. R. Reynolds & T. B. Gutkin (Eds.), *The handbook of school psychology* (pp. 796–828). New York: John Wiley & Sons.

Hardiman, R. (1982). White identity development: A process-oriented model for describing the racial consciousness of White Americans. *Dissertation Abstracts International, 43,* 10A. (University Microfilms No. 82-10330).

Helms, J. E. (1984). Toward a theoretical explanation of the effects of race on counseling: A Black and White model. *The Counseling Psychologist, 12,* 153–165.

LaFromboise, T. D. (1992). The interpersonal impact of counselor affinity, clarification and helpful verbal responses with American Indians. *Professional Psychology: Research and Practice, 23* (4), 281–286.

Lee, C. C., & Rotella, R. J. (1991). Special concern and considerations for sport psychology consulting with Black student athletes. Special Issue: Working with various populations. *Sport Psychologist, 5,* 365–369.

Manley, T. R., & Manley, E. T. (1978). A comparison of the personal values and operative goals of school psychologists and school superintendents. *Journal of School Psychology, 16,* 99–109.

Mannino, F., & Shore, M. (1985). The effects of consultation. *American Journal of Community Psychology, 3,* 1–21.

Meacham, M. L., & Peckham, P. D. (1978). School psychologists at 3/4 century: Congruence between training, practice and preferred role and competence. *Journal of School Psychology, 16,* 195–206.

Medway, F. J. (1982). School consultation research: Past trends and future directions. *Professional Psychology, 13,* 422–429.

Parsons, R., & Meyers, J. (1984). *Developing consultation skills.* San Francisco: Jossey-Bass.

Pipes, R. B. (1981). Consulting in organizations: The entry problem. In J. C. Conoley (Ed.), *Consultation in schools: Theory, research, and procedure* (pp. 11–33). New York: Academic Press.

Pryzwansky, W. B. (1986). Indirect service delivery: Considerations for future research in consultation. *School Psychology Review, 15,* 479–488.

Raffaniello, E. (1981). Competent consultation: The collaborative approach. In M. J. Curtis & J. E. Zins (Eds.), *Theory and practice of school consultation* (pp. 44–54). Springfield, IL: Charles C. Thomas.

Sabnani, H. B., & Ponterotto, J. G. (1991). White racial identity development and cross-cultural counseling training: A stage model. *Counseling Psychologist, 19* (1), 76–102.

Sue, D. W. (1990). *Counseling the culturally different: Theory and practice* (2nd ed.). New York: John Wiley & Sons.

Westermeyer, J., & Hausman, W. (1974). Cross-cultural consultation for mental health planning. *International Journal of Social Psychiatry, 20,* 34–38.

Westwood, M. J., & Ishiyama, F. (1990). The communication process as a critical intervention for client change in cross-cultural counseling. *Journal of Multicultural Counseling and Development, 18* (4), 163–171.

8

MULTICULTURAL CLASSROOM GUIDANCE

MICHAEL M. OMIZO AND MICHAEL J. D'ANDREA

WHAT IS THE PURPOSE OF EDUCATION?

One of the most debated issues in academia has been directed to the question: What is the purpose of education? Some people would readily respond to this question by saying that the primary purpose of schools is to help students gain the academic and career competencies necessary to make a living in the future. Other persons adopt a broader view of education, realizing that schools must also prepare children for "life" and not merely ready them to make a "living" in some future time (Jackson, 1987).

This latter view is more comprehensive than the former and, as such, is accompanied by a different set of expectations of what professional educators and counselors are obligated to do with their students. For those who believe that schools should primarily be designed to prepare individuals for the world of work, academic success and classroom behavior are popularly used as measures of the institution's effectiveness and students' progress.

In contrast, persons who hold the view that schools should play a broader role in preparing students for life are also interested in how well administrators, teachers, and counselors help children develop positive attitudes about themselves and others. Thus, these persons are equally concerned about the ways in which schools help students master a wide range of academic, cognitive, emotional, ethical, psychological, and social competencies that are necessary to lead meaningful, productive, and satisfying lives.

BEYOND "ACADEMIC-CENTRISM"

Clearly, promoting students' psychological health necessitates experiences that are different than those designed to stimulate children's intellectual development. With this in mind, it is suggested that professional educators and counselors, who focus on students' intellectual growth as the primary measure of educational success, are likely to neglect other equally important components of children's personal development. This typically results in less time being directed toward promoting students' psychological, emotional, social, and ethical growth and well-being.

Since the preparation and provision of daily instruction involves a great deal of a teacher's time and energy, school counselors are frequently called on to help foster various aspects of children's personal growth (such as their self-esteem and identity development). In responding to this professional responsibility, elementary school counselors have utilized a host of innovative guidance activities to stimulate students' social, moral, psychological, and emotional growth. Although these interventions focus on different aspects of children's development, they all share a fundamental commonality in that they are intentionally designed to nurture a sense of personal well-being during the elementary school years.

Over the past two decades, guidance activities designed to promote children's psychological and emotional growth have emerged as an integral part of elementary school education. Some of the factors that have contributed to a growing interest in the use of classroom-based activities to promote children's psychological well-being include:

1. An increasing acceptance of the notion that healthy adolescent and adult development is easier to achieve when one's childhood experiences have resulted in a firmly established sense of personal worth and competence

2. Escalating parental concern over their children's psychological development and ensuing support for school-based activities designed to stimulate students' personal well-being
3. Recognition that, due to the changing composition of U.S. families (e.g., both parents being employed, high divorce rates, the increasing number of single, female-headed households, etc.), most parents simply do not have the time and/or energy to provide the type of support and attention that are necessary to adequately meet their children's personal needs

The changing structure of American families—combined with an increased level of stress that parents experience as they attempt to cope with the unprecedented challenges of raising children in a rapidly changing, complex, modern society—causes many adults to reassess their expectations of teachers and school counselors. Accepting that these trends are likely to continue, it is suggested that parents will increasingly rely on these professionals to play a more formidable role in helping to promote their children's psychological health and personal well-being in the future. Thus, as we approach the twenty-first century, it is predicted that the general public will define educational excellence not only in terms of high test scores, which reflect students' academic proficiency, but also by the degree to which schools promote children's general psychological health and well-being.

BEYOND "CULTURAL-CENTRICITY"

As a result of research done in the field of multicultural counseling over the past 20 years, there has been a tremendous expansion in our understanding of the ways in which a person's cultural background impacts one's psychological development (Atkinson, Morton, & Sue, 1989; Lee & Richardson, 1991; Locke, 1992). Several experts emphasize that an accurate understanding of any student's psychological development and personal well-being can be achieved only when the cultural context in which one is reared is taken into account (Ivey, 1987; Ivey, Ivey, & Simek-Morgan, 1993; Pedersen, 1988). Such factors as one's cultural traditions, family values, the importance different groups place on formal education, and language differences clearly impact children's development in a variety of ways (Atkinson, Morton, & Sue, 1989; Lee & Richardson, 1991).

It is unfortunate that educators have generally ignored the impact of cultural/ethnic/racial diversity on children's development in the past. Although this has largely occurred out of a sense of benign neglect on the part of most educators, it has nonetheless resulted in teachers and counselors imposing their own values and attitudes on children whose cultural backgrounds are very different from their own. Consequently, "good students" are identified as those who are able (and willing) to assimilate into the public school milieu by generally divorcing themselves from their cultural traditions and identity.

Until recently, this sort of socialization was a hallmark of American education. However, with the tremendous influx in the number of elementary school-age children from diverse cultural groups in the United States during the 1980s and early 1990s, numerous persons have voiced concern regarding the negative effect this sort of ethnocentric approach to teaching and learning has had on children's academic achievement (Bullard, 1991; Omizo & Omizo, 1989), self-concept (Hilliard, 1991; Matthews & Odom, 1989; Phillips, 1984; Stafford & Hill, 1989), and personal development (Banks, 1991; Brandt, 1991).

As a result of this rising concern, many teachers and counselors have taken an activistic posture by serving as children's advocates within the school setting. In doing so, they have attempted to create changes to make teaching and learning more culturally relevant and respectful of a pluralistic student body. These efforts have fueled what is commonly referred to as the multicultural counseling and education movement (Atkinson, Morton, & Sue, 1989; Pedersen, 1988; Sleeter, 1991).

Despite the apparent need to incorporate multicultural counseling and education into the mainstream of this nation's public school systems, progress in this area has been impeded for numerous reasons. While numerous factors contribute to the lack of progress that has been made in this area, organizational resistance is identified as the single greatest barrier to infusing multicultural learning activities on a larger scale than already exists in this country's public schools.

Like individuals, most organizations resist innovative change. Schools are no exception to this phenomenon. The resistance to incorporate multicultural education goals and objectives into the general public school curriculum reflects a biased set of beliefs that many professional educators, administrators, and counselors hold regarding what should be taught and learned in our schools. In addition to these sort of pedogological biases, resistance to multicultural education is often reinforced by teachers who raise two reasonable arguments in their own defense.

First, many teachers simply present the reality of their professional lives. They emphasize that they are already overwhelmed with current expectations of what they should be doing in the classroom. "Why add to this overload," they argue, "by being required to infuse additional multicultural learning activities during the course of the regular school day?"

Others point out that their professional training did not adequately prepare them for multicultural education instruction. Given these conditions, many teachers feel that it is unfair to be expected to address an important concern such as multicultural education without being properly trained in this area themselves.

Accepting the reality of the current situation, it is suggested that counselors can do much to help bring about the types of institutional changes that are necessary in making education more culturally relevant for all students. Although there are a variety of ways school counselors might go about making these changes, this chapter examines the utility of using multicultural guidance activities to enhance students' awareness and knowledge of human diversity.

USING MULTICULTURAL GUIDANCE ACTIVITIES TO MEET CHILDREN'S PERSONAL NEEDS

Multicultural guidance activities can help children develop a sense of personal well-being as well assist them in becoming more respectful and sensitive to persons who are different from themselves. Both of these goals are very important considerations in helping children learn to become responsible citizens within the context of a culturally and racially diverse society. Such activities represent opportunities for personal development that, from the authors' viewpoint, should be an integral part of each child's educational experience during the elementary school years.

Viewed in this way, multicultural guidance activities are thought to hold tremendous potential in terms of assisting students in developing positive self-images, stimulating the acquisition of more effective social skills, and increasing their understanding of people who come from different racial, cultural, and ethnic backgrounds. Numerous researchers have reported that exposing children to multicultural issues during the elementary school years increases their awareness and tolerance of individual differences as well as positively affects other aspects of their psychological and cognitive functioning (Banks, 1991; Giroux, 1988; Hilliard, 1991; Pasternak, 1979).

Initial research findings suggest that multicultural education offers much promise in terms of promoting students' psychological well-being, but it is disturbing to note the lack of available resources in this area. If schools are to do a better job at promoting the psychological health and well-being of all students, much more work needs to be done to develop learning activities that are specifically designed to help youngsters learn to become more respectful and appreciative of human diversity.

With this backdrop in mind, the authors describe a set multicultural guidance activities that they developed and field tested among a culturally diverse group of fifth-graders. The activities presented in the following pages were designed to serve a threefold purpose. This includes helping students better understand how and why people from different backgrounds may think, feel, and/or act in ways that are similar or different from themselves; assisting them to develop more effective social skills; and fostering their sensitivity for the uniqueness of individuals who come from various cultural/ethnic groups. It was also noted that the following activities are particularly useful in helping children who are identified as being adversely affected by racism to develop positive self-concepts.

The guidance activities were scheduled once a week, requiring approximately 40 minutes per session and took place over a 16-week period. All of the activities were initially tried out with a culturally diverse group of fifth-grade students; however, the authors also found them to be effective with younger (i.e., third-graders) and older students (i.e., intermediate and secondary school-age youth). Slight modifications were made when using these activities with students in different grade levels, depending on the developmental needs and characteristics of the group. The activities used in this school counseling program were adapted from the work of several persons considered to be experts in the field (Fullmer, 1978; Pasternak, 1979; Omizo & Omizo, 1989).

Before describing the activities used in this school counseling program, it is emphasized that teachers can and should play an important role in providing these types of multicultural learning opportunities for their students. Professional school counselors were responsible for designing and testing out these activities in the classroom setting, but they also spent a great deal of time consulting with teachers to solicit their reactions and offer suggestions about ways in which they could use these activities with students in other classes. The authors acknowledge that multicultural education will become more fully incorporated into the total school curriculum when teachers are more supportive and confident about infusing these considerations into their daily instructional activities.

MULTICULTURAL GUIDANCE ACTIVITIES

Session 1: Name Tag Game
Give each child a large index card and ask each to print his or her name in the middle. Next, encourage the students to write four positive adjectives about themselves around their names. Then, in each corner of the card, ask each to write his or her (1) favorite food, (2) most enjoyable holiday, (3) favorite song or kind of music, and (4) dream country to visit. Divide the class into pairs and ask the children to interview and share the information listed on their partner's information card. Last, encourage all the students to share each other's information in front of the class. During this activity, the facilitator is encouraged to point out the specific types of information that highlight individual cultural uniqueness and similarities among the children.

Session 2: I Am
The counselor/teacher provides the children with drawing paper and asks the students to draw a picture of themselves. Tell the students to finish the sentence "I am..." with descriptors at least five times at the bottom of the picture. Next, ask the children to talk about their pictures and what they wrote about themselves. The facilitator is encouraged to point out any differences related to ethnicity or culture that may emerge from the students' self-descriptions in a

positive and supportive manner. Ask the children how they feel about their pictures and to discuss their characteristics with others. Finally, the counselor/teacher should display the pictures around the classroom so the children will have an opportunity to look and discuss them with each other after the activity is finished.

Session 3: Labeling

Select a concept that the children can easily understand (such as the opposites *boy* or *girl*, *tall* or *short*) but do not reveal the concept to the students. Then, divide the class into groups that reflect the specific concept in mind. For instance, if the concept is *girl* or *boy*, students should be put into groups according to gender. If the concept selected is *tall* or *short*, the children should be placed in groups according to height, and so on. Then label each of the groups as being "good" or "bad." Have the class guess the criterion by which the children in each group were labeled. Continue to do this with other characteristics.

Next, impose specific rules that determine what the "good" students can do and what the "bad" students are not allowed to do. For example, those children labeled "bad" cannot go out for recess and those who are labeled "good" can have 10 extra minutes of free play. Again, have the class guess the criterion that determined which students would receive certain privileges and which children were given punishments.

Then, discuss with the students how it felt to be labeled "good" or "bad," not knowing what the criteria were, not being in control of things, knowing that other children were placing values on them, and what their reactions were to sometimes being referred to as being "good" and other times being "bad" persons. Help the children explore the notions of stereotyping, prejudice, and value judgments. Finally, discuss the various reactions students had to this activity.

Sessions 4 and 5: Portrait Pluralism

Provide the children with drawing paper and have them draw pictures of themselves. Next, have them write their names below their pictures. Display their pictures around the classroom at levels where the children can reach. Explain to the class that during the next week, they may write something positive about their classmates on their pictures. Emphasize that everyone has good qualities and that their task is to discover as many positive characteristics about their classmates as possible. Tell the children that they should try to write something about everyone in the class. The facilitator should also write comments.

The class is encouraged to read the comments of other classmates during the week. After a week, divide the children into pairs and distribute their pictures to them. Have the pairs of students examine and discuss the information on the portraits among themselves. Then, ask the children to describe the comments written on their partner's self-portrait to the class. During the processing of this information, discuss how it felt to have others write comments on their pictures, if they felt differently toward any of their classmates than the comments that were written on their picture, if they were surprised at some of the good qualities written, and why they may not have been aware of their positive characteristics before.

At the conclusion of this activity, the facilitator should be sure to take time to point out those cultural factors that tend to influence the way people are sometimes viewed by others. It is important that the counselor/teacher use this time to note how people can easily stereotype others and to explain how the process of stereotyping influences the way individuals think and feel about persons from different cultural/racial/ethnic groups. Finally, have the students take their portraits home and share them with their parents.

Session 6: Cultural Warm Fuzzies
Arrange the students' chairs in a large circle so that everyone can see each other. Ask each child to think of something positive about each classmate that he or she can then share with the class. Ask for volunteers to express his or her compliments to each student. Have each student give his or her compliments to each peer.

Having done this with several students, the facilitator should point out patterns of the compliments that reflect various cultures and values that influence the types of compliments they gave to others. Finally, the counselor/teacher should lead a discussion about how being aware of the individual differences can help us to be more sensitive to how individuals feel and can increase our appreciation of everyone's uniqueness.

Session 7: Looking Beyond
Bring in pictures from magazines, books, and newspaper articles that portray men, women, and various ethnic, religious, and other minority groups in a negative manner. Divide the class into groups of three

or four children and have them analyze the pictures and articles. Have the groups discuss whether any stereotyping is suggested and if it exists, have them make a list. While the groups are presenting their discussions, make a list on the board of the stereotypes. Have the children discuss similarities and differences among the various groups. Highlight the limiting and negative effects of stereotyping, putting particular focus on cultural issues.

Session 8: Going Places

Divide the class into groups of four or five children so that each group represents a cross-section of the class relative to race, cultural/ethnic background, religion, and gender. Give each group a package containing pictures, information, and things from a different geographical part of the world (e.g., the Pacific islands, Asia, Africa, Middle East). None of the pictures should portray people or dwellings.

Next, the counselor/teacher instructs the students to refer to the pictures in responding to the following three tasks:

1. Describe the kinds of clothing that the persons residing in the places portrayed in the pictures are likely to wear.
2. Discuss the strengths of the people living in these places.
3. Describe the types of dwellings people would need to live in each area.

Having responded to these issues, encourge the children to discuss the following set of questions:

1. What would be the advantages of living there?
2. What would be the disadvantages of living there?
3. What do you think you would like best if you were to visit the place portrayed in the picture and interact with the people who lived there?

Give the students sufficient time to respond to these questions in their small groups before asking the groups to share their reactions with the entire class. When the group members are reporting to the class, the facilitator should try to probe the students to see if they can identify ways in which they may have allowed positive and/or negative stereotypes to impact their discussions. The counselor/teacher should also take time to have the students examine why some groups in the class may have had a difficult time talking about people who lived in different parts of the world. Finally, the facilitator should help the students examine reasons why members of the class had different reactions to the issues and questions presented in this activity. Particular attention should be directed to helping the children see how their own diverse backgrounds and life experiences influence the way they think about and react to people who are different from themselves.

Session 9: Advertising and Commercials
Bring in advertisements from magazines, newspapers, and recorded commercials from television. Present these materials to the class and have them discuss the following:

1. What ethnic group(s) is the advertisement addressing?
2. What types of people (men, women, children, senior citizens) are more likely to be influenced by the advertisement?
3. On which socioeconomic group in the United States is the advertisment focusing?
4. What are positive aspects of the advertisement?
5. What are negative aspects of the advertisement?
6. What types of ethnic stereotyping can you see are portrayed in the advertisement?

After discussing these questions with the entire class, have the students enact a television commercial that is specifically designed to appeal to one particular ethnic group. After the students have enacted this commercial, ask them what sort of modifications they could make to have it become more appealing to a diverse population of people. Finally, ask the students to reenact the commercial using the suggested modifications.

Session 10: We Are Unique
Take the class outside to walk in the schoolyard or to a nearby park. Point out the trees, flowers, grass, plants, birds, animals, leaves, and insects. After the counselor/teacher has done this with the students for a few minutes, ask the class what sort of things stood out for them along the way. The facilitator should focus on the uniqueness of the various things the students mention about the things they noticed on the walk as they return to the classroom.

Once inside the classroom, give the children some paint and paper. Then, ask them to paint something that caught their attention while they were walking and that they feel in some way reminds them of themselves. The counselor/teacher should emphasize the importance of painting a picture of something that reminds them of themselves, as the students will be asked to share their painting and thoughts with the rest of the class. As the children present their paintings to the class and explain why it reminds them of something about themselves, the facilitator takes time to point out each child's uniqueness and stresses the importance of appreciating the uniqueness of others.

Sessions 11 and 12: Creating a Country
Divide the class into groups comprised of four or five students. Provide a variety of art materials (paper, paint, crayons, felt pens) and inform the students that their task is to create a country. The country can be any size and shape and it can include rivers, mountains, lakes, forests, and so on. Once the country is created, the students must also create the inhabitants of their country.

Tell the children that they will have to discuss the language, dress, food, leisure activities, dwellings, art, government, educational system, and jobs for these people. At this point in the activity, students may need a brief explanation of what is meant by the term *culture*.

When the activity is completed, have each group describe its country, the inhabitants of the country the group created, and various aspects of the culture in which the people live. During this discussion, the counselor/teacher should ask the students how the country and people were created, what sort of conflicts persons in their country have and how they usually get settled, and how the culture in the different countries influences the way people act.

Session 13: My Dream Vacation
Tell the class that they have all won a vacation with all the expenses paid. What they must do is to write out their travel plans for this trip. Allow the students approximately 10 minutes to write their vacation plans. The children should be encouraged to include the types of places they would like to go, their preferred mode of transportation, types of accommodations, reasons for selecting a specific

destination, things they would take on the trip, the people they might invite to come along, and any other factors they can think of that would make this a perfect vacation. As the students describe what they have written, the facilitator should take time to point out similarities and differences in their vacation plans and how one's own cultural background influences the types of things people value and enjoy doing.

Session 14: Multicultural Art
Select an abstract concept such as *love, liberty, trust, peace,* or *justice.* Divide the class into groups of four or five children. Provide the students with paper and pens, crayons, and felt markers. Ask each group to draw a picture representing the specific concept chosen by the facilitator.

Have each group share its picture with the class and ask the group members to explain the drawing. The counselor/teacher should point out the uniqueness of each group's drawing and emphasize the fact that there is no incorrect representation of the selected concept.

Next, discuss the similarities and differences of the pictures with the students. Also, ask them to talk about different ideas that may have occurred among group members and how they were resolved. Finally, have the children consider ways in which their own cultural backgrounds influenced the type of picture they drew.

Session 15: Bidding for Values
Announce to the class that they will be having an auction. Items to be auctioned off include:

1. Honesty
2. Humility
3. Intelligence
4. Good health
5. Academic achievement
6. Ability to forgive
7. Having many friends
8. A trip around the world
9. Being loved
10. Self-confidence
11. Athletic ability

12. Ability to lose weight
13. A change in appearance
14. Being more organized
15. Stop procrastinating
16. Ability to express feelings
17. Movie videos
18. More toys
19. A new bicycle
20. Ice cream
21. Pizza

Each student is told to pretend he or she has $200.00 to spend at the auction. Instruct the students to look at the list of items to be auctioned and decide which of the items is most important to them. Items cannot be shared with other students and the highest bidder will receive the item being auctioned at that time.

Remind the students that they will have to keep track of their own money. Once their $200.00 is gone, they will not be allowed to continue in the bidding of other items. The counselor/teacher acts as the auctioneer.

After the auction has been conducted, discuss how the items were chosen, why they were selected, and how the students resolved conflicts during the bidding. Similarities and differences among the reactions of the class members should be noted and raised for discussion by the facilitator.

Session 16: Summary and Wrap-Up
The class meets to summarize the previous guidance activities. They are encouraged to share what they have learned, how what they have experienced by participating in this school counseling program influenced their lives, and raise any concern/question/comment they might have about the program at that time.

Research supports the use of these guidance activities in enhancing self-esteem and multicultural awareness (Omizo & Omizo, 1989). The students' teachers also reported that students seemed to have benefited from the multicultural guidance activities by exhibiting more appropriate social behaviors at school. They were also noted to demonstrate a better understanding of themselves and others after having participated in this program.

CONCLUSION

With the changing demography of American society, educators will most certainly continue to be challenged by the diverse needs, attitudes, values, and behavioral styles of children from different racial, ethnic, and cultural backgrounds. Schools are likely to respond to this social reality in one of two fundamental ways. On one hand, they can ignore students' cultural, racial, and ethnic differences and proceed to implement traditional instructional strategies. On the other hand, they can embrace cultural diversity as a reality of modern society and incorporate innovative learning activities that increase students' multicultural awareness by encouraging them to become more tolerant and respectful of individual differences.

In considering the press for greater cultural sensitivity in our public schools, two additional points must also be taken into consideration. First, it is expected that the current level of interest and demand for curriculum changes that affirm respect for cultural, ethnic, and racial differences will increase during the 1990s. Second, given the present state of curriculum materials (e.g., textbooks) and the nature of teacher training in this country (which often lacks a multicultural perspective), it will undoubtedly take time for schools to make the transition to incorporating a multicultural orientation in the content and process of American education.

Accepting these two points, it is stressed that counselors can play a crucial role in this transitional period by advocating for the infusion of multicultural guidance activities at the elementary school level.

REFERENCES

Atkinson, D. R., Morton, G., & Sue, D. W. (1989). *Counseling American minorities.* Dubuque, IA: William C. Brown.

Banks, J. A. (1991). Multicultural education: For freedom's sake. *Educational Leadership, 49* (4), 32–36.

Brandt, R. (1991). A caring community. *Educational Leadership, 49* (4), 3.

Bullard, S. (1991). Sorting through the multicultural rhetoric. *Educational Leadership, 49* (4), 4–7.

Fullmer, D. W. (1978). *Counseling: Group theory and system.* Cranston, RI: Carroll Press.

Giroux, H. A. (1988). *Teachers as intellectuals: Toward a critical pedagogy of learning.* Granby, MA: Bergin & Garvey.

Hilliard, A. G. (1991). Why we must pluralize the curriculum. *Educational Leadership, 49* (4), 12–13.

Ivey, A. E. (1987). Culture intentionality: The core of effective helping. *Counselor Education and Supervision, 26,* 168–172.

Ivey, A. E., Ivey, M. B., & Simek-Morgan, L. (1993). *Counseling and psychotherapy: A multicultural perspective.* Boston: Allyn and Bacon.

Jackson, J. (1987). *Straight from the heart.* Philadelphia, PA: Fortress Press.

Lee, C. C., & Richardson, B. L. (Eds.). (1991). *Multicultural issues in counseling: New approaches to diversity.* Alexandria, VA: American Association for Counseling and Development.

Locke, D. C. (1992). *Increasing multicultural understanding: A comprehensive model.* Newbury Park, CA: Sage.

Matthews, D. B., & Odom, B. L. (1989). Anxiety: A component of self-esteem. *Elementary School Guidance and Counseling, 24,* 153–159.

Omizo, M. M., & Omizo, S. A. (1989). Art activities to improve self-esteem among Native American children. *Journal of Humanistic Education and Development, 27,* 167–176.

Pasternak, M. G. (1979). *Helping kids learn multi-cultural concepts.* Champaign, IL: Research Press.

Pedersen, P. (1988). *A handbook for developing multicultural awareness.* Alexandria, VA: American Association for Counseling and Development.

Phillips, R. H. (1984). Increasing positive self-referent statements to improve self-esteem in low-income elementary school children. *Journal of School Counseling, 22,* 155–163.

Sleeter, C. E. (Ed.). (1991). *Empowerment through multicultural education.* Albany, NY: State University of New York Press.

Stafford, W. B., & Hill, J. D. (1989). Planned program to foster self-concepts in kindergarten children. *Elementary School Guidance and Counseling, 24,* 47–57.

9

COORDINATION OF COUNSELING SERVICES IN A CULTURALLY PLURALISTIC SCHOOL ENVIRONMENT

JOHNNIE H. MILES

Emphasis on pluralism in counseling grew out of the civil rights movement of the 1950s and 1960s as minorities demanded increased access and quality treatment by mental health professionals. These actions brought special attention to the social needs and legal rights of minority groups. Then, in the 1970s, a new influx of immigrants and refugees brought about significant changes in population statistics. Hodgkinson (1985) stated that America was changing so rapidly that by the year 2000 one out of every three people would be a minority individual.

Consider the following scenario, which further illustrates the dynamics of a shifting population. According to Gibbs (1991), California in 1980 was 76 percent white. With its Hispanic population growing by more than 70 percent and its Asian community by 127 percent, the state in 1990 was 57 percent white. The schools also reflected those shifts. Inglewood High School in California, for example, was 90 percent white 20 years ago, 90 percent black 10 years ago, and 48 percent Latino in 1991.

It is imperative that school counselors factor in pluralism both in planning and making provisions for the delivery of services. Counselors are often considered the professionals who know the most about students, their needs, and available resources, and are therefore expected to identify, refer, and link resources on behalf of the student (Cole, 1987). The increase in diversity presents both a challenge and an opportunity for schools and counselors to broaden traditional areas of service. Coordination, the role of the counselor that is least discussed and rarely taught in training programs, is most applicable in providing avenues for counselors to assure equity in human service delivery systems in pluralistic environments.

The purpose of this chapter is to provide background information and strategies on the coordination role of school counselors as they function in a pluralistic environment. Since coordination has not been explored as fully in the literature as other roles, this chapter presents a brief explanation of coordination and describes the types of activities or strategies which may be used by counselors. To illustrate the practical contributions of coordination to counseling, numerous vignettes and case scenarios are interwoven throughout the chapter.

COORDINATION AS COUNSELOR ROLE

School counselors have traditionally fulfilled a number of functions as part of their role (Terrill, 1990). There have been numerous attempts by professional groups to produce role statements that would adequately describe the functions of school counselors. It was not until 1966 when an interdivisional committee of the American Personnel and Guidance Association—the Association of Counselor Education and Supervision and the American School Counselor Association (ACES-ASCA)—issued a statement on elementary counselors that some widespread agreement on roles was achieved. It was the ACES-ASCA statement that identified the primary roles of elementary counselors as counseling, consulting, and coordinating (ACES-ASCA, 1966). The American School Counselor Association, 25 years later, adopted a similar role statement for school counselors at all levels that specified again the three generally recognized helping processes used by the counselor as counseling, consulting, and coordinating (ASCA, 1990).

Coordination is defined as "the process of managing various indirect services which benefit students and being a liaison between school and community agencies" (ASCA, 1990). Coordination is a time-intensive aspect of the school counselors's job but plays a very special part in facilitating the total counseling program. It is a means for organizing and managing counseling programs while delivering quality services to clients, preventing overlap, conflict, and duplication of programs.

In a pluralistic environment, coordination takes on a new dimension of responsibility as reflected in the comments of an experienced counselor in the Washington, D.C., metropolitan area:

> I am a seasoned counselor and am accustomed to assessing student populations to determine service and program needs. The past five years have been more of a challenge for planning because the student body is continually changing. As a result, I find it necessary to provide more orientation, consulting, and in-service for parents, teachers, and counselors; I collect more information about cultures and culture-specific organizations not previously contacted; and we offer programs and services never before considered (e.g., clothing bank). Much of what we do at school is like running a social service agency on an emergency basis. While it has been more work to perform all these tasks, it has also been very rewarding. To see the immediate results of your work is a benefit that most counselors never witness.

This counselor was verbalizing what most recognize, which is that schools are truly multicultural and therefore may require a different approach to the way counselors work. Schools are made up of many groups, sometimes differentiated by their racial or ethnic identities (Latino, American Indian, Middle Eastern) or by their orientations based on religion (Jewish, Adventist, Moslem); language (Spanish speaking); values (independent or group orientation); gender; or even sexual orientation. Membership in or an identity with a particular cultural group exerts significant influences on lifestyles, language, coping patterns, beliefs, traditions, behavioral orientations, prejudices, and values (Axelson, 1993; Gladding, 1988; Lee & Richardson, 1991; Sue & Sue, 1990). The contemporary counselor will also be confronted by numerous other issues or presenting problems such as substance abuse, runaways, dropouts, reconstituted families, AIDS, and teenage pregnancy, which are not cultural but will require culturally sensitive management. In a pluralistic environment, the basic issue becomes awareness and understanding by the counselor of the role cultural context plays in shaping needs and behaviors of clients that are exhibited in the school setting (Sue & Sue, 1990). This level of understanding allows the counselor to consider the individual and the two cultures within which the student operates (Vernon, 1993).

COORDINATION STRATEGIES

The strategies counselors use to accomplish the role of coordination in any situation are basic ones. They include planning, scheduling, program development, program evaluation, public relations, research, collaborating, consultation, and organizing. Counselors use these tools to plan and facilitate their efforts and those of other school personnel in ways that promote growth and development of clients. Thus, coordination provides the framework through which counseling and consulting roles are performed and establishes a medium through which all student services specialists may work together as a team (Baruth & Robinson, 1987; Gibson, 1990; O'Bryant, 1991; Kamen, Robinson, & Rotter, 1985).

Contextual factors may influence the use of a particular strategy. For example, counselors have generally concentrated on working with students in schools and looked to the family as support of those efforts. Today, counselors focus their work both on the student in school and on strengthening the family so it can provide support to the child and the school. The first approach to work was based on tradition and the latter on seeing the client in context. In Alexandria, Virginia, a destitute immigrant family received from their children's school the food, clothing, furniture, and money needed to get settled in the area. A Hyattsville, Maryland, mother received money from the school community to help bury a son. According to Buckley (1993), schools have usually directed needy families to social service offices and neighborhood clinics or provided information referrals. Today, these schools are getting involved, offering services directly or organizing the school community to provide the services. Services such as parenting seminars and workshops on opening checking accounts, budgeting, or how the American system works have been well received by new immigrants. Some schools operate clothing and food banks, teach English classes, and recruit culturally different parents as volunteers. These services have not been limited to immigrants but are made available to all who need them. Principals at schools who provide such help see immediate results through increased participation by parents and support of their children in school activities.

The primary organizers of these types of efforts are the school counseling staff. They recognize a need and amass the resources to respond to that need, generally through their role as coordinators. The counselors' actions resemble the kind of social networking described by Speck and Attneave (1973) in their work on retribalization of American Indians following hospitalization and/or as an alternative to hospitalization for mental health related conditions. Speck and Attneave (1973) discussed the interrelationships and interdependency of family, neighborhood, friendships, work associations, and community agencies with the person in therapy and the value of incorporating all groups in interventions that enable clients to cope and restore support systems. A number of studies have indicated that clients who participate in network therapy have significantly less contact later with mental health agencies (LaFromboise & Fleming, 1990). Their work has major implications for counselors in a pluralistic environment. It will assist counselors in seeing clients in context to their culture and community and in broadening counselors' perspectives on the resources available in providing support for clients.

Coordination covers such a vast range of activities that it is often broken down into categories, such as external and internal activities (Engelkes & Vandergoot, 1982). External activities are those that link school counselors with professionals and individuals significant in the life of the client to facilitate collaboration and ease of service delivery. The activities described above are examples of external coordination activities. Other external activities might include outreach to the family in seeking their involvement in schools. Many culturally different groups have not had positive experiences with schools or may not know how the school functions. Perhaps developing strategies that include personal contact might be more effective than the note home to parents. The face-to-face encounters may inform parents about the school and how it functions, the role of teachers and counselors, and the relationship between students and teachers.

According to Sue and Sue (1990), there are some cultural groups for which psychology and counseling are unknown quantities and who would therefore not likely access the services. Counselors would need to reach out to these groups and gradually teach them about the value of counseling and mental health services. In situations like this, it would be helpful to have a staff member or a parent volunteer who is a representative from the group to assist in establishing initial contact. A similar type of outreach is recommended for African American and Hispanic parents, two groups with low participation rates in traditional school activities. Perhaps counselors need to review program offerings to determine if topics are of equal interest to the groups being recruited. Conducting a needs assessment of parents, teachers, and students would provide information to make programs relevant to the target audience.

Referral is another coordination strategy for meeting the needs of clients. It is a process of transferring an individual client to another person or agency for specialized services (Cole, 1987). Occasionally, counselors may find it appropriate to refer because clients' needs exceed the counselor's level of competency, or have goals incompatible with the counselor's values, or have emotions or biases that limit the ability to serve clients (Cormier & Cormier, 1991). There may also be situations in which culturally specific factors make a referral a most appropriate strategy. Consider, for example, a young male Saudi with a career-related concern being assigned to a female counselor. Due to well-defined sex roles within his culture, the placement may not be in his best interest, particularly if he is a strong adherent to the culture of his country. In this case, referral may involve reassigning the client to a male counselor or seeking appropriate assistance outside the school. This example is not intended to suggest that only same-gender or same-race counselors can be effective. It does, however, provide support for the concept that student services professionals should reflect the rich diversity of their constituencies.

In referring a client in a pluralistic environment, care should be taken to identify those agencies in the community that specialize in culture-specific services and/or have established reputations of providing effective services on an equitable basis to all clients. Networking with other professionals is an important process for becoming knowledgeable about the nature and quality of resources in the community.

Internal coordination refers to activities performed by counselors to assure the smooth operation of the in-school counseling program. The counselor may carry or share responsibility for coordination of all guidance activities. In this role, the counselor may be called on to coordinate the work of school psychologists, social workers, and others, as well as to facilitate interagency referrals. This approach allows counselors to keep abreast of what is being done or not being done and to assure that all clients get the services needed. It becomes the counselors' role to assess climate issues that are negative for culturally different groups and take the steps necessary to communicate the concern to appropriate authorities. The coordination role would necessitate counselors being mindful that the nature of programs delivered within the school would be focused toward inclusion rather than exclusion of students. Such a role as coordinator in a diverse climate requires counselors to engage in proactive strategies for program design and delivery.

COORDINATION IN A PLURALISTIC ENVIRONMENT

It is evident that coordination in a pluralistic environment requires a culturally sensitive mindset. Chunn, Dunston, and Ross-Sheriff (1983) strongly suggested that practitioners have specific training with people of color during their preparation programs to develop an understanding of the real-life experience of their clients. Cultural sensitivity must be developed through intense training, experience, and involvement with culturally different groups (Pedersen, 1988).

If counselors expect to be successful in any of their roles in a pluralistic climate, they must first examine their attitudes and personality styles and how these characteristics influence their behavior with culturally diverse clients (Peterson & Nisenholz, 1991); be able to communicate, verbally and nonverbally, through their attitudes and behaviors that they accept, respect, and value culturally diverse clients (Vernon, 1993); and be aware of their skill limitations and be sensitive to the necessary conditions that may impact the referral of culturally different clients (Sue & Sue, 1990). With all these elements in place, counselors may then be perceived by clients as catalysts for human growth and development, understanding, and change (Thompson, 1992).

COORDINATION AT DIFFERENT LEVELS

How might the coordination function be performed at elementary/ middle and high school levels? Each setting and level at which a counselor works will present clients with developmental needs and characteristics, institutional goals, and operating procedures that may differ. These dissimilarities may call for application of somewhat different dimensions of role and function by counselors (Baruth & Robinson, 1987). Two case scenarios will be utilized to illustrate some additional ways coordination and other roles may be performed. Although the focus here is on coordination in a pluralistic environment, the techniques and strategies might also be used in different environments.

Case Scenario: Elementary

An elementary counselor, working with a fifth-grade student of Middle Eastern background referred by the teacher, discovers that the student's behavior had shifted drastically over a four-week period. Her homework, which had previously been turned in on time, was currently not being submitted or turned in with careless errors. She had been withdrawing from contact with other classmates, especially the females. The student appeared lonely and often opted to have lunch in the classroom rather than eat in the cafeteria.

Through talking with the teacher (consulting), the counselor discovers that the student was capable but seemed distracted. She learns from a cafeteria worker that the student enjoyed sitting with her classmates but often moved or became quiet when they started to discuss weekend activities (consultation). The counselor confirmed, in discussions with the client, that the student felt her classmates spent far too much time talking about clothes, makeup, and boys (counseling). The counselor further recognized that the student was experiencing typical developmental needs of wanting to be accepted but could not participate in any of the activities that were natural for the other girls. She collaborated with the teacher and organized a "lunch bunch" group for the girls from the class (planning). They chose topics of discussion that were more general in nature, read and discussed books, and explored the cultures represented in the group. In addition, the teacher followed up and planned several discussion sessions over lunch that covered general topics in which all female students could participate; designed more in-class group activities; and often assigned a question or a problem to be considered and answered by teams over lunch. The student began to submit homework assignments and became more involved again with students in her class.

The counselor was able to use her knowledge of the Islamic culture in collaborating with the teacher. An appropriate strategy was designed to include the student in class-relevant activities to meet basic developmental needs without interfering with cultural beliefs.

Case Scenario: Secondary

A high school counselor was supervising a practicum student from a nearby university and had learned during the interview that the student was fluent in Spanish. One of the first clients assigned to her was a female client of Hispanic origin (coordination of practicum and internship). The practicum student noticed immediately that the client was not comfortable speaking in English and she quickly switched to Spanish. The student counselor was able to quickly establish rapport using the client's native language (counseling).

The following day, the client returned with five friends who made appointments for counseling. The practicum student was informed by the client that this was the first time students like them had someone who understood them (consulting). The practicum student and the supervising counselor set out to determine how many students were in the school for which English was not their primary language and how many would be interested in counseling if it were available to them (needs assessment/coordinating).

The results revealed a significant number of students speaking Vietnamese and Spanish, with a few speaking Chinese and Farsi as native languages. The counselor and practicum student used the findings to plan and initiate a group for nine Spanish-speaking tenth-grade young women on social adjustment—a top-identified need on a counseling needs survey of Hispanic students (research, program planning, coordination). The group was co-facilitated by the practicum student and a counselor with some training in Spanish (counseling). The counselor, convinced that students from different cultures would access counseling services more frequently if there were representatives from their own culture or persons who spoke their language, set out to confront the problem.

In surveying the school division, she found one counselor fluent in French, and five who had taken classes in Spanish during college (research/coordination). She found a sufficient number of external interpreters but they did not have backgrounds in counseling or psychology. Due to potential ethical issues, she pursued another avenue to meet needs of students. She developed a report of her research and sent it to the central office with a recommendation for filling the next vacancy with a counselor fluent in Spanish (research, coordination). She contacted the local university and requested two practicum students for the next semester, one fluent in an Asian language and the other a male fluent in Farsi, because most of the Middle East students were male (coordinating, consulting). The university was able to grant the request for a practicum student fluent in an Asian language but did not have one currently enrolled who could speak Farsi (coordinating). Feeling energized about her accomplishments, the counselor worked with a task force that designed several parenting sessions to orient new arrivals to schooling in America; several sessions on parenting skills; an orientation program for new students; and a recruitment program to bring Hispanic, Korean, and other culturally different students into the peer helper training program (program planning, coordinating, training).

From these two case scenarios, it becomes apparent that counselors do participate extensively in coordinating activities, even though their actions are not always identified as such (e.g., planning, scheduling, follow-up). The nature of coordination, as demonstrated by these two cases, was influenced by developmental needs of the client group, leadership skills of the counselor, and the existence of a school climate that allowed flexibility in the work of the counselor.

The counselor, as coordinator, would be particularly concerned about external and internal issues that affect the school and community. Trends such as population shifts, changes in leadership, changes in educational goals and practices in the school, and the social, economic, and political climate in the community all have the potential to impact on parents and community agencies. Each of these variables has significant implications for guidance and counseling programming. For example, one counselor in an urban school on the East coast reported that Asian membership, primarily Vietnamese, increased by 15 percent in one year in her school. That change necessitated a quick response on her part to collect and understand information regarding the new students' culture. It required a slight shift in the focus of orientation programs for new students, the design and delivery of an in-service for teachers on Vietnamese culture, and the addition of a group for newcomers on understanding American culture. As demonstrated by this situation, a change in one aspect of the school system necessitates changes in others.

CONCLUSION

This chapter has explored the multifaceted dimension of coordination as a role for counselors with emphasis on implementing the role in a pluralistic environment. Counselors are responsible for coordinating their own work as well as the work of others. And in a pluralistic climate, counselors may have to do more, do it differently, and do it better to assure that all their clients are served.

Counselors must determine when classroom guidance programs will be scheduled, how much individual counseling to conduct, how much time to spend on record keeping, how much emphasis to place on diversity planning, and how to work with teachers and administrators to integrate pluralistic philosophy into policy and curriculum planning. In essence, each counselor must coordinate to accomplish expected roles and functions. The extent to which counselors perform the coordination role will depend on their perception of the importance of the role, size, and number of counselors in the school, the availability of other human services professionals, and the amount of diversity represented in the school and community. The more diversity that exists, the more visible the need for action.

Coordination within a pluralistic environment can be a challenging and exciting experience. Counselors who are well trained will be prepared for the experience, and the school and their clients will benefit.

REFERENCES

ACES-ASCA Committee on the Elementary School Counselor. (1966, February). The elementary school counselor. *Personnel and Guidance Journal, 44,* 658–661.

American School Counselor Association. (1990). *Role statement: The school counselor.* Alexandria, VA: American School Counselor Association.

Axelson, J. A. (1993) *Counseling and development in a multicultural society.* (2nd ed.). Pacific Grove, CA: Brooks/Cole.

Baruth, L. G., & Robinson, E. H. (1987). *An introduction to the counseling profession.* Englewood Cliffs, NJ: Prentice Hall.

Buckley, S. (1993). Schools increasingly fill breach to help immigrant parents. *The Washington Post,* April 11.

Chunn, J. C., Dunston, P. J., & Ross-Sheriff, F. R. (1983). *Mental health and people of color.* Washington, DC: Howard University Press.

Cole, C. G. (1987). Referral and collaborative working. In C. W. Humes (Ed.), *Contemporary counseling* (pp. 187–201). Muncie, IN: Accelerated Development.

Cormier, W. H., & Cormier, L. S. (1991). *Interviewing strategies for helpers.* Pacific Grove, CA: Brooks/Cole.

Engelkes, J. R., & Vandergoot, D. (1982). *Introduction to counseling.* Boston: Houghton Mifflin.

Gibbs, N. (1991, November). Shades of difference. *Time,* 66–70.

Gibson, R. L., Mitchell, M. H., & Higgins, R. E. (1983). *Introduction to counseling and guidance.* New York: Macmillan.

Gladding, S. T. (1988). *Counseling: A comprehensive profession.* Columbus, OH: Merrill.

Hodgkinson, H. (1985). *All one system: Demographics of education—Kindergarten through graduate school.* Washington, DC: Institute for Educational Leadership.

Kamen, M. C., Robinson, E. H., & Rotter, J. C. (1985). Coordination activities: A study of perception of elementary and middle school counselors. *Elementary School Guidance and Counseling 20,* 97–104.

LaFromboise, T. D., & Fleming, C. (1990). Keeper of the fire: A profile of Carolyn Attneave. *Journal of Counseling and Development, 68,* 537–547.

Lee, C. C., & Richardson, B. L. (Eds.). (1991). *Multicultural issues in counseling: New approaches to diversity.* Alexandria, VA: American Association for Counseling and Development.

O'Bryant, B. J. (1991). Getting the most from your counseling program. *NASSP Bulletin, 75* (534), 1–4.

Pedersen, P. (1988). *A handbook for developing multicultural awareness.* Alexandria, VA: American Association for Counseling and Development.

Peterson, J. V., & Nisenholz (1991). *Orientation to counseling* (2nd ed.). Boston: Allyn and Bacon.

Speck, R., & Atteneave, C. (1973). *Family networks: Retribalization and healing.* New York: Random House.

Sue, D. W., & Sue, D. (1990). *Counseling the culturally different: Theory and practice.* (2nd ed.). New York: John Wiley and Sons.

Thompson, R. (1992). *School counseling renewal: Strategies for the twenty-first century.* Muncie, IN: Accelerated Development.

Terrill, J. L. (1990). Toward the 1990's: Emerging themes in school counseling. *NASSP Bulletin, 74* (527), 84–88.

Vernon, A. (1993). *Counseling children and adolescents.* Denver, CO: Love.

10

ACCOUNTABILITY IN A CULTURALLY PLURALISTIC SCHOOL SETTING

ARLEEN C. LEWIS AND SUSANNA HAYES

INTRODUCTION

All school counselors face the major responsibility of offering effective services to all of their constituencies, including students, teachers, parents, and administrators. However, surveys indicate that counselors at all levels are faced with student/counselor ratios that are far above recommended ranges (Myrick, 1987), making this task a formidable one. It is not unusual to find ratios of 1:650 or even 1:1,400 in the public schools. Needless to say, such workloads are extreme and may cause the counselor to experience feelings of being overwhelmed. Furthermore, if among the students there are newly arriving immigrants or individuals from differing cultural backgrounds—such as Native Americans, African Americans, Asian Americans, Hispanic Americans, or Americans of Middle Eastern ancestry—the counselor's responsibilities become even more challenging. Those who are struggling to acquire new skills, a new language, new friends, and new successes must be high on the counselor's list of priorities. In essence, the quantity of counseling needs in an increasingly diverse school setting can stand as a formidable challenge to the school counseling professional.

Community expectations for the counselor are also important. Given the relative newness of school counseling as a manifestation of ancient traditions of where elders nurture youth, there are hopes that counseling services will produce confident, understanding, emotionally mature, motivated, responsible, and career-ready youth. Internalizing these expectations further contributes to a feeling of tremendous pressure for the counselor.

This chapter will present some options to the dilemmas school counseling professionals face. Topics such as strategic planning, program evaluation, time management, and accountability may seem to some to belong within the realm of school administration; however, this chapter will place these concepts firmly within the counselor's domain. The accountability process can help to set priorities, organize and manage time, garner support from the community and school, and provide a data-based rationale for programs and services. Importantly, the results of accountability studies may also provide justification for the additional staff, facilities, and equipment needed to meet the ever-growing challenge of cultural diversity in many schools. The chapter begins with a definition of accountability and its relationship to program evaluation and research. The remainder of the chapter will focus on the basic elements of accountability, including needs assessment, program development, and evaluation within a culturally pluralistic school setting.

WHAT IS MEANT BY ACCOUNTABILITY?

Krumboltz (1974) has defined *accountability* as the set of procedures that assist in organizing information in order to make decisions. In other words, to be accountable means to have evidence or documentation to support counseling practice. *Accountability, research,* and *program evaluation* are related terms. *Research* is a process of hypothesis testing under strictly controlled conditions that advances knowledge. Although extremely important for the development of the discipline, research is less relevant to counselor accountability efforts than is program evaluation (Burck & Peterson, 1975). Program evaluation is the process of making judgments about specific programs or intervention systems, particularly in the context of program goals and objectives. An advantage of using a program evaluation model as part of accountability efforts comes from the goal setting and planning that are an intrinsic part of program evaluation. When accountability is approached from a developmental perspective, the following questions become relevant:

1. What is the current status of the school counseling program?
   a. What services are provided for all groups of students, especially those newly enrolled and/or culturally different?
   b. How does the school and broader community assess the counseling program?
2. What are the current needs in the school as perceived by the counselors, teachers, administrators, students, and parents that can be addressed by a comprehensive counseling program?
3. What program goals will meet those needs?
4. What additional programs and services should be instituted?
5. How are we measuring progress toward achieving our goals?
6. Who is asked to participate in the evaluation of our programs and services?

PROGRAM EVALUATION

Program evaluation is a process for making qualitative judgments about counseling services that includes a number of interrelated steps or activities. The model that will be presented in this chapter includes the following components:

1. Forming advisory groups
2. Assessing counseling program needs
3. Developing program goals and objectives
4. Collecting data for decision making
5. Evaluating and modifying programs accordingly

The accountability movement of the 1960s and 1970s called for counselors to identify effective strategies to enhance student development in educational, social, and vocational areas (Gysbers & Henderson, 1988). These strategies were based on the philosophy, goals, and objectives of counseling programs. Although measures of effectiveness are part of accountability, programmatic accountability is far more comprehensive in scope than the studies of counseling effectiveness reviewed by Tyler (1969). Parents, administrators, community leaders, teachers, and students need to be included in programmatic assessments. The observations and specific recommendations from all of these groups are critically important if counselors are to remain focused on community- and student-based priorities. This is particularly important for the priorities of culturally diverse communities and students, which may differ significantly from a traditional educational focus.

Forming Advisory Groups

Unless counselors consistently invite community members from *all* cultural groups to participate in planning and implementation for the counseling program, there is a strong likelihood that the real needs of those groups may be misrepresented or overlooked (Davis-Russell, 1990). The inclination to focus on universal needs of a population rather than group-specific needs is a common tendency among counselors (Sue & Sue, 1990)—one that may further emphasize the needs of the white students over those of the ethnically diverse students.

The politics of fair and adequate representation of culturally diverse populations is seldom obvious, but it is important that school counselors become aware of the major concerns all families have regarding their children. These would include universal notions such as providing for young people and ensuring that they are educated. Models for working with representational committees exist in such programs as Johnson-O'Malley and Title V of the Indian Education Act. When federal funds were set aside for the particular educational needs of Native American students, school districts were required to include their communities in the design, monitoring, and staffing of programs (Fuchs, 1970). Increased communication between community members and school personnel in these programs was facilitated by evening meetings, potluck suppers, and early morning breakfasts. Community participation in school events was encouraged by career fairs, peer helping programs, student/class contributions, and community service. Such events and activities represented a transition from centralized management of the school to more democratic models. Parents who felt uncomfortable speaking at school board meetings were empowered to share their ideas on behalf of their children at these activities and events.

Assessing Counseling Program Needs

Well-publicized public forums that solicit direct input from parents and the community at large are a practical way to build and maintain community-counselor communications. The inquiries need not focus on complex issues. Rather, it is helpful to draw attention immediately to student needs. The following questions may be used to initiate and structure the group discussion:

1. What are the primary needs of students that counselors should address in (a) elementary schools, (b) middle/junior high schools, and (c) high schools?
2. How can counselors help parents meet the challenges associated with raising their children?
3. How can counselors assist teachers and other school staff who are involved in academic programs?

Responses vary greatly depending on how regularly the school has requested parent and community participation in accountability sessions. It is also important that issues such as timing, location, and child care be arranged for the convenience of the community (Ascher, 1987). Social interaction of persons attending can be encouraged by creating a friendly atmosphere. School personnel can welcome and talk informally with community members, offer refreshments, and arrange circular seating formations. The discussion can be recorded on flip charts or computerized overheads. If the latter form is used, every person can receive a record of the discussion.

Another way to gain detailed input is through interviews with parents and community leaders. The following questions may serve as a guide for interviewing a sample of parents from the cultural/ethnic groups served by the school:

1. What would you like your child to learn in school that he or she is not learning now?
2. What would you like for teachers, administrators, and students to know about your child's cultural/ethnic background?
3. How can the counselor help your child to become a better student?
4. What activities outside of class will help your child enjoy being at school? Are there any cultural/ethnic activities that we could stage here at school?

5. As a parent, how do you want to be included in your child's educational activities?
6. What programs would you like the counselors to provide for parents?

Sometimes the parents' first language will be other than English, and a translator will be needed to assist the counselor during the interview. It is also helpful to offer either school-, home-, or work-based interviews. The long-term value of this input is greatly enhanced when it is ongoing and there is evidence that the counseling program has responded to the recommendations made during the interviews (Ascher, 1987). For many ethnically diverse parents, the newness of participation in decision making about school programs may be uncomfortable. Due to negative experiences in their own schooling, many ethnic minority parents may avoid active involvement in their children's schooling.

Given the often infrequent use of counseling services by individuals from culturally/ethnically diverse groups (Sue & Sue, 1990), it is advisable for counselors to provide them with detailed and specific information about counseling as a helping service. If possible, an informational video could clarify the major goals and methods used in counseling. Informative and attractive brochures, translated as needed, would also assist in expanding general awareness of counseling.

Student Surveys and Interviews

As an adjunct to more traditional instruments for assessing counseling program needs, it is often helpful to obtain information on student self-esteem. This type of data provides a much more personal view of the needs of students than can be derived by asking them to generate lists of needed programs or activities. The counselor can elicit direct information from students based on their views of themselves rather than relying on extrapolations from academic performance or participation in extracurricular events. Opportunities for students to address direct questions about feelings of personal pride, self-worth, and interpersonal competencies provide directional cues for developing counseling services. For example, when students indicate they have few friends among peers who are culturally different from themselves, school personnel are alerted to examine how institutional scheduling and programming may reinforce tendencies for students to resegregate themselves. Counselors who document students' feelings of isolation and alienation have a basis for formulating large and small groups that facilitate positive cross-cultural sharing among students. Students who express discouragement or fear about their futures alert counselors to the need for increased positive attention and nurturance beyond what is received in classes or through informal exchanges among peers. Furthermore, genuine interest in the growth of students encourages expression of feelings and hopes that arise from thoughtful introspection.

Table 10–1 provides an example of a checklist that the chapter authors designed to provide information on self-esteem and school. It can easily be administered to a sample of students as part of the needs assessment process.

It is also useful to conduct follow-up interviews with a sample of students. Interviews provide greater depth of information and are also useful for obtaining information from students who are reluctant to complete survey instruments. They are also a valuable way for a counselor to make personal contact with students and establish credibility. The following series of questions can be used as a guide for structuring such interviews:

Questions Regarding Mobility

1. How long have you attended this school?
2. What schools did you attend before coming here?

Questions Focusing on Students' Relationships

3. How many friends do you have at school?
4. How are your friends helpful to you?
5. Do you have friends from other cultural groups?
6. Which teachers are your friends?
7. Do some teachers or friends discourage you about school?
8. Have you ever talked with a counselor or other adult at school about things that bother you?
9. Would talking privately with a counselor about things that bother you be helpful?

Questions Regarding the Curriculum

10. What classes do you like and what do you like about them?
11. What classes do you believe are not helpful to you?
12. What do you need to learn that is not taught at school?

TABLE 10–1   Student Survey

Your counselors need to know how you are doing. Please complete this form by checking the way you think about each item.

	Like Me	Not Like Me
1. I usually do the right thing.	———	———
2. I'm as good as everybody else.	———	———
3. Things often bother me.	———	———
4. It's hard to talk in front of a group.	———	———
5. I often feel left out of things around school.	———	———
6. Kids usually pick fights with me.	———	———
7. No one pays much attention to me at school.	———	———
8. There are many times I feel like leaving school.	———	———
9. No one pays much attention to me at home.	———	———
10. Most people understand the way I feel about things.	———	———
11. I make up my mind without too much trouble.	———	———
12. People at school expect me to work too hard.	———	———
13. My parents don't really care what I do at school.	———	———
14. I know I can get help at school if I want it.	———	———
15. Most of the time I get what I need without much trouble.	———	———
16. I don't think school will help me in my future.	———	———
17. My friends often want me to skip school with them.	———	———
18. Almost every day something bad happens to me.	———	———
19. I usually get blamed for things others do.	———	———
20. Lots of times I feel like running away.	———	———

13. Do you learn about different cultures and ethnic groups in your classes?
14. What can counselors do to help you learn better?
15. Are you able to participate in making decisions about what happens at school?
16. What is the relationship between what you do in school now and your plans for the future?
17. If you weren't in school, what would you like to be doing?

Developing Program Goals and Objectives

After the counselor has completed the needs assessment, in consultation with the advisory group, it is important to establish goals and objectives for the counseling program. These need to be based on the outcome of the community discussions, interviews, and surveys. Goal setting is extremely important, for this is the blueprint that will guide the development of the counseling program. It is important that this blueprint be culturally sensitive and responsive to the needs of a diverse student body.

Collecting Data for Decision Making

A critical element in the accountability process is to provide evidence that can be used to make decisions about programs and activities. There are four general types of data that can be used to provide the information needed to evaluate programs and establish accountability:

1. Time logs
2. Outcome data
3. Constituent feedback
4. Case studies

Time Logs
Time logs are a structured way of keeping records about how the counselor spends his or her work time. In a national survey of accountability practices of school counselors, Fairchild (1993) found that 94 percent of the counselors who collected some type of accountability information kept this type of data. Time logs will not help in evaluating the quality of counseling programs and services, but the information obtained in this way can serve many useful proposes.

It is very helpful in time management and goal setting to have accurate information on what activities are consuming our time. This information can be used to set priorities and establish needs for clerical support services and so forth. In addition, much of the work of the counselor may not be highly visible, and data about the numbers of students seen and the variety of services provided are very useful when responding to questions about the counseling program. In a culturally diverse setting, these types of data provide information about how counseling services are distributed across groups of students. Are certain groups more likely to receive counseling services? If so, what could account for this difference?

Figure 10–1 provides an example of a time log that can be used on a daily basis to record these types of data. It is provided as an example, however, and is not expected to meet the individual needs of every counselor. Since every counseling program is somewhat unique, this form can be adapted to a variety of programs. In modifying the form, the following points are suggested:

- Record direct service contact. Include time and numbers of students (e.g., 1½-hour group; 6 students).
- Make the system efficient. The less time you spend recording daily activities, the more time you will have for direct service.
- Stay current. As time goes by, activities will slip from memory. Maintain a weekly summary that provides a visual representation of main events and services.
- Code clients by *gender, cultural group,* and/or *ethnicity.* By comparing these figures with the population data for your school, you will be able to determine if there are gaps in appropriate services for the persons or groups who may have specific needs.
- Develop categories for recording data that follow logically from your overall program objectives. This will facilitate analyses of your time and annual report writing.

Outcome Data
Outcome data include the quantitative information that verifies that programs and services have had the planned effect. These data are collected after the intervention, but it is critically important that decisions on the type of data to be collected be made at the time that program goals are established. Otherwise, it may be difficult to obtain the particular information needed. An example illustrates this

point. One of the problem areas that has been identified by a needs assessment concerns a program to decrease the number of fights between groups of Hispanic and white youth on the basketball courts in the morning before the start of school. The planned intervention is to provide a series of classroom guidance activities that focus on conflict management and the development of cooperative relations between the ethnic groups in the school. Data about the number of fights before and after the classroom program would be very valuable in assessing the impact of the program on fighting between the two groups. However, unless plans were made to use these data in advance, the baseline data necessary to make these comparisons would not be available. Pre- and postprogram data are a meaningful way of determining student growth and program effectiveness. It would also be helpful to gather participant statements about what they found to be most helpful. Other examples of outcome data include grades, test scores, behavioral observations, or the student survey data on self-esteem collected as part of the needs assessment.

Constituent Feedback

Constituent feedback refers to interview or survey information obtained from students, teachers, administrators, and parents concerning attitudes toward the counseling program and the impact of its services. Although some people have questioned the value and accuracy of such data, it seems logical that the opinions that constituents hold about counseling programs and services will always be relevant in decision making. Laing (1988) has suggested that the quality of the self-report data can be improved by following a few general principles in setting up questionnaires:

- The respondent needs to be clear about what information is being requested.
- The information needs to be available to the respondent.
- The respondent needs to be willing to provide the information.
- The counselor must accurately interpret the information provided.

Excellent examples of questionnaires designed for parents, students, teachers, and administrators are provided by Rye and Sparks (1991). The text also provide examples of instruments that can be used to evaluate the counselor by the principal.

FIGURE 10–1   School Counselor Daily Activity Log

	COUNSELING					COORDINATION					
	Student	Group	Family	Class Guid.	Career Dev.	Peer Interv. Program	Administrative Activity				
							Mtgs.	Prep.	Paper	Sched.	
7:00											
7:30											
8:00											
8:30											
9:00											
9:30											
10:00											
10:30											
11:00											
11:30											
12:00											
12:30											
1:00											
1:30											
2:00											
2:30											
3:00											
3:30											
4:00											
4:30											
5:00											

TOTALS

Date _____

FIGURE 10–1 *(Continued)*

CONSULTATION				MISCELLANEOUS			
Parent Contact	Teacher Consult.	Class Obs.	Super-vision	Apprais. Activity	Phone	School Activity	Staff Devel.

Case Studies

Case studies are extensive analyses of individuals that can be used to present examples of atypical situations or to provide greater depth of information about individual students than is obtained from other sources of data. Case studies are particularly important in culturally diverse school settings because the importance of cultural and ethnic variables in a young person's situation may not be apparent with more conventional types of data collection and analysis. For example, a review of the counselor time log data may reveal that the African American students within the school are underserved by the school counselor. Case studies of a small number of African American students could help the counselor achieve a greater understanding of how he or she is perceived within the African American community and what needs must be addressed before students will be comfortable seeking out counseling services.

Evaluating and Modifying Programs Accordingly

After data on the counseling program have been collected and analyzed, it is very important to review the information in light of the program goals and objectives. Is there evidence that the counseling program is meeting the needs of students and the school community that were identified through the work of the counseling staff and advisory group? If the data-collection process has not yielded evidence that this is the case, it may be necessary to make modifications in the existing program in order to meet those needs. For example, if certain groups appear to be underserved, special outreach programs may need to be developed in order to make counseling services more accessible.

Counseling program development is never a finished process. The needs of students and the community change and programs must be modified accordingly. The program evaluation model presented in this chapter details a process that can be used as a blueprint for creating programs that respond to the changing needs of students.

CONCLUSION

Accountability is central to addressing the challenges presented by cultural diversity in schools. Individual differences between students that develop as a result of class, ethnicity, gender, or cultural background may result in different counseling program needs for these young people. Even in those cases where students with different cultural backgrounds have similar needs, the effectiveness of a particular counseling intervention in meeting those needs may vary for students from one cultural group to another. Counseling professionals are responsible for ensuring that programs and services reach all students in the school community. Accountability efforts make this task easier by helping assess needs, establish priorities, and obtain relevant data about services.

The school counseling literature contains a variety of helpful materials for getting started in accountability efforts. For example, Lewis (1983) has provided a list of resources that may be useful in evaluating school counseling programs. Such materials provide an excellent starting point in the accountability process. Once again, it must be emphasized that being accountable does not require sophisticated research designs and analyses. Rather, accountability involves listening to the needs of a wide range of constituencies, developing goals and objectives based on those needs, collecting appropriate data, and making decisions that further the continued development of counseling programs.

REFERENCES

Ascher, C. (1987). *Improving the school-home connection for poor and minority urban students.* Institute for Urban and Minority Education. New York: Teachers College, Columbia University.

Burck, H. D., & Peterson, G. W. (1975). Needed: More evaluation, not research. *Personnel and Guidance Journal, 53* (8), 563–569.

Davis-Russell. (1990). Incorporating ethnic minority issues into the curriculum: Myths and realities. In G. Stricker (Ed.), *Toward ethnic diversification in psychology education and training* (pp. 171–177). Washington DC: American Psychological Association.

Fairchild, T. N. (1993). Accountability practices of school counselors: 1990 National Survey. *The School Counselor, 40* (5), 363–374.

Fuchs, E. (1970). *Curriculum for American Indian youth.* Office of Education, Department of H.E.W., Washington, DC: U.S. Government.

Gysbers, N. C., & Henderson, P. (1988). *Developing and managing your school guidance program.* Alexandria, VA: American Association for Counseling and Development.

Krumboltz, J. D. (1974). An accountability model for counselors. *Personnel and Guidance Journal, 52,* 639–646.

Laing, J. (1988). Accuracy of self-reported activities and accomplishments of college-bound students. *Journal of College Student Development, 29* (4), 362–368.

Lewis, J. D. (1983). Guidance program evaluation: How to do it. *The School Counselor, 31,* 111–119.

Myrick, R. D. (1987). *Developmental guidance and counseling: A practical approach.* Minneapolis, MN: Educational Media Corporation.

Rye, D. R., & Sparks, R. (1991). *Strengthening K–12 school counseling programs: A support system approach.* Muncie, IN: Accelerated Development.

Sue, D., & Sue, D. W. (1990). *Counseling the culturally different.* New York: John Wiley and Sons.

Tyler, L. E. (1969). *The work of the counselor.* Englewood Cliffs, NJ: Prentice Hall.

PART IV

PROFESSIONALISM AND THE CULTURALLY RESPONSIVE SCHOOL COUNSELOR

Professionalism refers to the commitment a school counselor has to assure the delivery of high-quality service. Changing population demographics challenge school counselors to reassess their professional attitudes and behaviors and take action to ensure that they have the awareness, knowledge, and skill to deliver quality services to all students. Chapter 11, which concludes the book, offers direction for developing professional competencies to become a culturally responsive school counselor.

11

MULTICULTURAL LITERACY: IMPERATIVES FOR CULTURALLY RESPONSIVE SCHOOL COUNSELING

COURTLAND C. LEE

INTRODUCTION

Implicit in all the issues considered in this book is an ongoing process through which school counseling professionals acquire the competencies to be culturally responsive service providers. To become this type of counselor, it is necessary to engage in activities that will facilitate personal growth and professional development. In this final chapter, aspects of professionalism that are imperative for the development of multicultural literacy in school counseling are discussed.

The American School Counselor Association, in its position statement on cross/multicultural counseling (1988), lists a number of strategies that counselors may use to promote the concept of cultural diversity within the school environment. The authors who have contributed to this current book have attempted to provide a broad perspective on the strategies listed in that position statement. If such strategies are to be successfully operationalized, however, school counselors and related professionals must have the competencies to do so. Significantly, counseling scholars have advocated the development of multicultural counseling competencies for a number of years (Carney & Kahn, 1984; Lee, 1991; Pedersen, 1988; Sue & Sue, 1990; Sue, Bernier, Durran, Feinberg, Pedersen, Smith, & Vasquez-Nuttal, 1982). Recently, Sue, Arredondo, and McDavis (1992) provided an updated conceptual framework in which to consider the promotion of such competencies. This framework is a call to all sectors of the profession to acknowledge the growing influence of cultural diversity on counseling theory and practice. It conceptualizes the development of competencies along three dimensions: beliefs and attitudes, knowledge, and skills.

These three dimensions are discussed in this chapter within the context of school counseling in a culturally pluralistic society. Although they are considered separately, these dimensions are interconnected and establish a competency framework for multicultural literacy in school counseling practice.

Examining Attitudes and Beliefs

It is imperative that a school counseling professional begin the process of becoming culturally responsive by examining personal attitudes and beliefs. This should start with an exploration of how his or her own culture has impacted on personal psychosocial development. Of particular importance is a careful examination of the factors that contributed to the formation of his or her ethnic identity during childhood and adolescence. It is of considerable significance that he or she consider the role that cultural heritage and ethnic customs played in shaping early personality characteristics.

It is equally important to evaluate the forces that may have shaped the development of one's early attitudes and beliefs about people from different cultural backgrounds—for example, recalling the messages received from parents and other significant others during one's formative years about people who were "different."

After carefully examining key relationships between culture and early psychosocial development, a counseling professional should consider how the issues associated with diversity from childhood and adolescence impact on current attitudes and beliefs. Specifically, one must evaluate how personal attitudes and beliefs about young people from culturally diverse backgrounds may facilitate or hamper counseling effectiveness. A culturally responsive school counseling professional, therefore, explores personal issues and questions in an attempt to find out how his or her heritage, values, and possible biases might impact on students who are culturally different in a helping relationship.

Self-exploration leads to self-awareness, which is crucial in developing a set of personal attitudes and beliefs to guide multicultural counseling practice. A culturally responsive school counselor is sensitive to cultural differences because he or she is aware of his or her own culture.

Acquiring Knowledge

It is imperative that a culturally responsive school counselor has a knowledge base from which to plan, implement, and evaluate his or her services to the school community. First, he or she must have an understanding of how social and political systems operate with respect to their treatment of culturally diverse groups. For example, he or she should have an understanding of the potential impact of environmental variables such as poverty and racism on the psychosocial development of young people.

Second, a counselor who is responsive to diverse student groups acquires specific knowledge and information about the cultural backgrounds of these young people. This should include specific knowledge about the history, experiences, customs, and values of culturally diverse groups. From such knowledge should come an understanding of specific cultural contexts and how they may influence the mastery of important developmental tasks during childhood and adolescence.

Third, underlying all of this, a culturally responsive school counselor must have clear and explicit knowledge of traditional counseling theory and practice related to the school setting. Especially important is a basic understanding of human development across the life span. It is only then that a counselor who is grounded in such traditions can fully appreciate the necessity of potential cultural variation in traditional school counseling practice.

Building Skills

It is imperative that a culturally responsive school counseling professional build a repertoire of relevant skills. He or she should be able to use counseling strategies and techniques that are consistent with the life experiences and cultural values of students from diverse backgrounds. In order to develop and implement such skills, however, a school counseling professional must first have awareness and knowledge related to issues of cultural diversity.

A culturally responsive school counselor should have the skills to establish rapport in individual and group counseling with culturally diverse students. These should include the ability to engage in a variety of both verbal and nonverbal helping activities with students. A counselor should also be able to modify his or her theoretical approach when cultural differences become a source of conflict and misunderstanding between themselves and students.

A culturally responsive school counselor should also be able to use various individual and group multicultural counseling techniques to promote student development. Such techniques should incorporate culture-specific materials and ethnic dimensions to foster self-concept, promote interpersonal relationships, and improve problem-solving/decision-making ability among students in a pluralistic educational environment.

Planning, implementing, and evaluating career development programs for culturally diverse students is another important skill area. A counselor should have the ability to orient students to the world of work within the context of values, interests, and abilities developed in diverse cultural contexts. This should include promoting possible interest among students in careers in which members of culturally diverse groups have been underrepresented.

Finally, a culturally responsive school counselor should have the ability to consider the dynamics of culture/ethnicity when interpreting data from standardized tests and other assessment tools. He or she should be able to recognize possible cultural bias in assessment instruments and consider this when making educational decisions about students from culturally diverse backgrounds.

It seems obvious that school counselors have a responsibility to themselves, their clientele, the profession, and society at large to ensure that they have the competencies to adequately address the challenges and opportunities of cultural diversity. Population demographics make it essential that school counselors be adequately prepared to focus on the needs, interests, and issues related to the developmental tasks of children and youth from many racial/ethnic backgrounds.

SUGGESTIONS FOR PROMOTING PROFESSIONAL DEVELOPMENT

To be effective and culturally responsive, it is necessary for counselors to engage in activities that will promote professional development. For example, continuing to actively explore the richness of one's own culture would be an important way to enhance both personal growth and professional development. Enrolling in a multicultural counseling course in a university counselor training program would be another. This would be a good way to become acquainted with current multicultural theory, research, and intervention methods. Short of formal university coursework, advocating for comprehensive in-service professional development programs on multicultural counseling conducted in work settings would be another way to be introduced to important issues and recent trends. Likewise, attending professional meetings, workshops, and conferences that address multicultural issues would provide important ideas for enhancing school counseling programs.

Active involvement in state, regional, and national professional associations and organizations that promote cultural diversity in the school setting and beyond can also promote personal development. Such involvement provides a professional network for advancing multicultural knowledge and skills.

School counseling professionals should also consider enhancing their personal growth and professional development by reading the literature and exposing themselves to other forms of artistic expression from culturally diverse groups. A great deal of information about lifestyles, customs, traditions, language patterns, values, and history, and their impact on human development and personality can be gained from such activity.

Finally, school counseling professionals should go out and experience cultural diversity first hand. There is a limit to how much can be learned about culturally different groups of young people from classes, workshops, or books. Much more can be learned by actually being among children and adolescents from diverse backgrounds and interacting with them in their cultural environments. Plans should be made to visit with young people at family gatherings, religious services/ceremonies, ethnic festivals, and so on. Such in vivo experiences can raise levels of awareness, increase knowledge, and provide important dimensions to empathic style in counseling interventions with culturally diverse students.

What is the underlying imperative in all of this for present and future school counseling professionals? It is to be able to view each student as a unique individual while, at the same time, taking into consideration his or her common experiences as a child or teenager (i.e., the developmental challenges that face all young people regardless of race or ethnicity) and the specific experiences that come from his or her cultural background. In addition, the counselor needs to make a constant effort to be in touch with his or her own personal and cultural experiences as a unique human being who happens to be a helping professional.

CONCLUSION

As we look ahead to the twenty-first century, it is becoming clear that a new American culture is emerging—a universal culture where diversity and pluralism are accepted hallmarks of the society. Young people who represent diverse world views characteristic of this pluralism, and who are the future leaders of this new national order, are now maturing and developing their abilities and interests. They will need guidance in this developmental process from counseling professionals whose expertise includes a sensitivity to human diversity and the skills to help develop talents within the context of cultural realities. These young people will also need to see professional role models whose attitudes reflect the notion of strength in diversity and who have the knowledge and skill to make cultural pluralism a lasting national concept. When all of this is taken into consideration, school counseling professionals have the potential to be on the cutting edge of making a culturally diverse society a reality.

REFERENCES

American School Counselor Association. (1988). *Position statement on cross/ multicultural counseling.* Alexandria, VA: American School Counselor Association.